Things You Should Know

André Klopper

Copyright © 2014 André Klopper

All rights reserved.

ISBN-10: 1501004980
ISBN-13: 978-1501004988

DEDICATION

I thank Bets. Without her, I am no one. With her, I can do everything. All through the book my wife Bets had been an inspiration and great support.

ACKNOWLEDGMENTS

This book would not have been possible without the help of my friend and collaborator in so many things, Jan Smith. From ideas and suggestions and hours of discussions Jan has helped make this book what it is. Thank you and Darryl Black for your editing work and Ashik Ali for the wonderful front cover.

Since I majored in economics I have kept up to date with what is going on around the world. In the beginning it was work related but later it was just my fascination about the subject. This book builds on the work of many excellent historians and economists, who I cited in the bibliography. I am very grateful for their scholarship, which allowed me to develop my own interpretation of events.

Also By André Klopper

The Immigrants
How To Write
Stone Bird Country

André Klopper

#	Chapter	Page
1.	Introduction	8
2.	Humanity	15
3.	Economics 101	24
4.	Banking	43
5.	The Consumer Exploitation	49
6.	The Evolution of Money	57
7.	The Gold Standard	65
8.	Capitalism	79
9.	Globalisation	86
10.	Why are Some Countries Poor?	101
11.	The Federal Reserve	109
12.	World Bankers	113
13.	The Rise And Fall Of The United States	121
14.	Japan	133
15.	China	143
16.	Asia & Australasia: The Dynamic Region	154
17.	The Philippines and Sri Lanka	162
18.	Singapore	166
19.	Europe	169
20.	The Politicians	173
21.	Government Statistics	181
22.	The Ponzi Schemes	186
23.	Derivatives	191
24.	The Banking Crises	196
25.	Cycles and Trends	213
26.	Economic Recessions	223
27.	Currency Wars	254
28.	Oil Reserves	257
29.	Facts and Figures	263
30.	Wall Street	272
31.	Collapse	276
32.	Hyperinflation or Deflation?	284
33.	The Global Currency Reset	290
34.	Machine Intelligence	297
35.	Disposition Towards Money	301
36.	Important Things	314
37.	Changing Course	321
38.	The Meltdown: Why, When, Where and Who	333
39.	What Should We Do?	345
40.	Keywords	356
41.	Bibliography	368

André Klopper

1. Introduction

This book is to help you to prepare for what lies ahead, and for you to decide with this knowledge how to implement such personal steps to adapt. It will liberate and embolden you to take action. This book is mostly about economic beliefs and how they affect policies. But to establish the link between the crisis and those beliefs, one has to unravel what has happened. This book is not a "whodunit," but there are important elements of the story that akin to a good mystery.

How did the largest economy in the world go into freefall? What policies and events triggered the great downturn of 2008? Finding root causes is like peeling back an onion. Each explanation gives rise to further questions at a deeper level: perverse incentives may have encouraged short sighted and risky behaviour among bankers, but why did they have such perverse incentives?

Understanding the coming financial meltdown is the first step towards protecting your wealth. To save is easier than you think, so much of what we currently buy we can easily do without. It will also show you how to be successful by changing your predisposition towards money.

"The secret of freedom lies in educating people, whereas the secret of tyranny is in keeping them ignorant' - Robespierre

Hope: a feeling of expectation and desire for certain things or events to happen. Who does not want a good standard of living, decent health facilities, the chance of travel and similar or better opportunities for their children?

For the last thirty years most people are in the mode of wishful thinking that everything is, and will continue to, be all right. The great depression is a thing of the past never to be repeated again. They believe the present civilisation is exempt from the normal cycles of rise and fall which happened long before the industrial revolution began.

Is this true? Why do we believe this? Because we are optimists by nature, we look at the staggering the potential of new technologies to improve our lives. The drive from developing countries for a more modern lifestyle will create all sorts of opportunities and economic progress. But is it true?

André Klopper

The single-minded focus on making money influenced our belief that economic growth benefits human kind and the greater the growth the more widespread the benefits.

We see ourselves as masters of creation who are able to go anywhere, achieve almost anything, with nothing but the laws of physics to stand in our way. We believe we are in control and that the environment is merely a set of resources, to be used at will, energy is abundant and cheap, growth can continue without limit and science, technology and engineering can secure the future.

Over the last few decades we have created an artificial demand for growth at any cost, without any evidence that it makes us happier. The quickest way to prosper was to ride the wave of progress, using more energy, more resources and more technology than our ancestors.

Why do we chase brand names, slogans, fashions, technology, all the in-things, the red-hot conversation topics, the deafening chorus of got-to-have-it-now mentality which quickly fades to white noise in the background that we are dimly aware of?

This is all out of fear of being forgotten, since being forgotten makes life seem pointless.

Things You Should Know

The average 21,000 days of our lives are reduced to maybe twenty memorable days that over time also succumb to nothingness.

People wish to leave a mark, an impression on earth that they were here. They don't want to pass through the world as if they never existed, immediately forgotten in the haze of our daily routine.

Therefore we are deceitful animals. We skilfully, weave a false front, often extensive and complex, fact and fiction in a delicate blend to accentuate the good and acceptable, and to hide the bad.

Those who don't shape the future, or don't leave a trail of their journey here on earth, can only hope.

However, hope is not a course of action. Some people play lotto in the hope that the winnings will change them, bringing happiness and meaning into their lives. But money isn't equal to happiness, the latter needs to be found within us. Only by choosing to be happy with what we already have, can we hope to enjoy a sense of happiness and contentment in our lives.

Some people need luxury like others need air. An expensive car, nice clothes and a bit of good service are simply a must for them to feel they exist.

People feel they need to stand out, to escape from the homogeneity of the masses. We are no longer defined by what we do, but what we own. We want to create an image of ourselves through all that we have purchased, to hold a placard of ourselves up to the world that says 'this is me'. It comes from the evidence of consumerism, superficiality and greed, the origin of all lies and pretence.

Like it or not, money is part of our very being. We worry more about money than anything else. We fight with our spouses and families more about money than anything else. We spend more of our waking hours earning and spending money than doing anything else.

Money isn't the goal itself but if you don't have a solid workable plan, then the lack of money can take over your life. It is a great irony: If you don't think smart about money, you'll wind up thinking about money all the time. But once you got your money sorted out, you can think a lot less about your finances and a lot more about things that are important.

It may seem like money buys happiness but it is not true as happiness comes from within us and our dealings with other people. Money is only one kind of wealth, a mark of secondary success.

Primary success arises from our character and is measured in terms of the contributions we make, integrity, honesty, hard work and compassion for others.

Therefore don't judge people by the size of their wallets but by the size of their hearts and the quality of their character. There are people out there that have focus in life they are pushing hard to improve themselves and the things around them.

Marcus Aurelius said:

'Always bear this in mind that very little indeed is necessary for living a happy life.'

Talking about his ranking as the world's richest man, Gates said, "I wish I wasn't. There is nothing good that comes of that."

Teddy Roosevelt once said: "The most important single ingredient in the formula of success is knowing how to get along with people."

People want analysis to say the economy will improve in the future, not to say it will get worse. They don't want to hear about the Internet bubble, the Asian currency crisis, the Russian government bond default, even if all of these extreme events have been compressed into a fantastically short space of our financial history.

It is a universal desire for people to only want to listen to good news. It is an unfortunate effect of group think that most authorities are afraid to voice an unpopular opinion because they are afraid of being wrong and losing face. The same is true for academics, many of whom have been shunned and ridiculed by their peers for voicing a radical idea. Being proved right years later, perhaps after their death is of little consolation.

People don't want to listen to bad news therefore it takes guts to yell 'fire' when so few people believe you, because they can't even smell the smoke or don't want to. We have to treat the truthful economist and financial analyst, as doctors who provide honest diagnosis and not people who are there to cheer you up.

One thing is for certain the middle class is not going to be the same as it once was. The middle class know they have a roof over their heads and it is not public shelter and they know where their next meal is coming from, and that isn't from the soup kitchen. That is all about to change.

I am not forecasting Armageddon but if you are observant you'll notice a nearly complete absence of straight talk from policy makers about ways to solve these increasingly complex problems or about the crisis about to face us.

The Chinese symbol for crisis is a

combination of two symbols: the symbol for danger and the symbol for opportunity. The danger is what everybody sees; the opportunity is never quite as obvious as the danger, but it is always there.

Norman Vincent Peale said. "Believe in yourself. Have faith in your abilities. Without a humble, but reasonable confidence in your own powers, you cannot be successful or happy."

2. Humanity

The tough challenges that face our society are as old as society itself: crime, disease, poverty and war. It is an undeniable fact that for most of our history, human beings treated each other terribly. Conflicts were frequent. With each conflict, more and more human beings were killed.

Luckily for us the decline of senseless killing clearly means the world is becoming a more civilised place. With each passing decade in the civilised world, we worry less and less about being killed by a fellow human being.

Everyone wants to eliminate poverty, the root of violence, hunger disease homelessness and pollution. Yet when people read in the newspapers about the majority of the population who live in this poverty due to the lack of employment, poor education, insufficient infrastructure, huge debt, poor governance and rampant corruption, they think there is nothing they can do about it.

Some people think poor people are just lazy and must snap out of it and find work. What do you think? Most of the poor people are far from lazy as every day is a struggle which requires constant problem solving, and no matter how bad their lives are, it's just too painful to risk more failure.

Muhammad Yunus stated:

"Poverty does not belong in civilized human society. Its proper place is in a museum."

Every winter between 25,000 and 30,000 people die from cold in one of the most developed countries in the civilized world, the United Kingdom, most of them being elderly and vulnerable people. The British conservatives point to the vicious cycle of welfare dependency from one generation to another stating, the social welfare system which was originally designed to help support the poorest in society is now trapping them in the very condition it was supposed to alleviate. Handouts of food and healthcare simply mire the poor deeper into their dependence on the State.

Things You Should Know

How do you destroy a community/society?

Vladimir Lenin statement- "Corrupt the young, get them away from religion. Get them interested in sex. Make them superficial, destroy their ruggedness. Get control of all means of publicity and thereby: Get the people's mind off their government by focusing their attention on athletics, sexy books and plays, and other trivialities.

Divide the people into hostile groups by constantly harping on controversial matters of no importance. Destroy the people's faith in their natural leaders by holding up the latter to ridicule, contempt and obloquy. Always preach true democracy but seize power as fast and ruthless as possible.

Encourage government extravagance, destroy its credit, and produce fear with rising prices, inflation and general discontent. Foment unnecessary strikes in vital industries, encourage civil disorder and foster a soft and lenient attitude on the part of government towards such disorders.

By specious argument cause the breakdown of the old moral values: honesty, sobriety, continence, faith in the pledged word, and ruggedness. Cause the registration of all firearms on some pretext, with the view of confiscating them leaving the population defenceless."

André Klopper

When Emperor Ashoka of India attacked and destroyed the peaceful land of Kalinga more than two thousand years ago, he found himself in the midst of the bloodshed and rubble, horrified at what he had done. To his credit, he spent the rest of his life trying to atone for it. He renounced his greed for lands to conquer and dedicated himself to the eradication of violence and poverty, both economic and spiritual.

He urged his people towards peace and generosity, pleading with them to have respect, be dutiful and pure. He travelled through his empire, meeting with the people, learning about their problems, and doing his best to teach them self-reliance and compassion for one another.

This is his creed which is engraved in pillars all over India: "What I desire for my own children- I also desire for everyone, welfare and happiness both in this world and the next."

With these principles he transformed himself from the worst kind of bipolar thinker, attacking and massacring anyone who opposed him, into the embodiment of synergy. He became an energetic social innovator alongside his people, devising roads and roadhouses, universities, irrigation systems, temples, and a new thing called a hospital. He banned violent punishment for crimes. He never went to war again because he resolved conflicts in the spirit of *dharma*. He was the first to institute laws for the protection of minorities and promoted tolerance for all religions.

Hilary Clinton wrote:

We must stop thinking of the individual and start thinking about what is best for society... We are all part of one family. To raise a happy, healthy, hopeful child it takes all of us. Yes, it takes a village.

What do we gather from all this? We must become interdependent people who are fully self-reliant and fully responsible to each other at the same time. This could best be explained by Switzerland. Many of us think of Switzerland as a peaceful, prosperous land with pretty mountains and great chocolate.

As a nation, Switzerland is an unquestioned success story. Swiss workers lead the world in efficiency. The Swiss per capita income is on top of the rankings. The Swiss government is among the most effective and transparent in the world.

But Switzerland shouldn't even be a nation. Nothing about Switzerland is favourable to nationhood. Geography is against it: Swiss live on different sides of the massive Alps, enjoy a few natural resources, and have no access to the sea. Language is against it: French is spoken in the west, German in the north and east and Italian in the south and they are dived between Protestants and Catholic.

The unification began with General Guillaume Henri Dufour who led his forces in the Napoleonic wars. He said to his men, not to be angry or revengeful but prove their courage as generous soldiers. Protect the defenceless; do not destroy anything unnecessarily; in a word, conduct yourselves in such a manner as to win respect.

Dufour's extraordinary care for the wounded enemy soldiers and his generous terms won the admiration of the rebels and helped unite Switzerland. In 1863 he presided over the first Geneva Convention, which created the International Red Cross.

After the civil war the Swiss engineered a national government unlike any other in the world. They adopted a system of direct democracy and any citizen can challenge the legitimate laws through a petitioning process on which the entire electorate votes on the issue.

When the Swiss knew their voice would be heard, a remarkable transformation overtook the country and peace became a governing principle. Other contributing factors include the educational system; the law no longer requires any ethnic group identity, only individuals; all individuals, religions, and languages are respected.

Things You Should Know

At the end of 2011 Switzerland had an unemployment rate of only 3.2 percent.

Five hundred years ago, Christopher Columbus noted in astonishment in his diaries how the native people of America held no personal property, but everybody in the society shared everything that was owned. If you asked a person to give you anything that seemed to be theirs, he observed, they invite you to share it with love in their hearts.

Forty years ago, Martin Luther King warned that: "We must rapidly begin the shift from a thing-orientated society to a person-orientated society. When machines and computers, profit motives and property rights are considered more important than people, the giant triplets of racism, militarism and economic exploitation are incapable of being conquered. A nation can flounder as readily in the face of moral and spiritual bankruptcy as it can through financial bankruptcy."

This is not advocating that we should give up all material possessions but merely suggesting that if we all become just slightly less "thing-orientated", if we all put, a little more care and thought into the impact of things that we buy, our lives may not only be a lot better for it, but we may also save the planet for our children and their grandchildren.

André Klopper

The antidote for chasing after material things is to belong to a caring community. Community is a collection of people who interact with one another in the same environment. Belonging is the reward of a strong social community, if there is no belonging there is no community. The community as a whole will benefit by the cooperation of all its parts, while the individual will find in his associations the advantages of the help, the sympathy, and the fellowship of his neighbours.

What does this all mean? The hallmark of a strong community is when members feel they belong and all participants believe the community brings them together. The community provides a sense of value to the members.

Trust is critical; for people who don't trust each other will struggle to form a community. To achieve trust and confidence you need a firm foundation of understanding and patience. By carefully listening to each other people find respect, which is important in reinforcing belief in the community.

Stories are part of communication; fables are passed down from generation to generation, each one providing a moral message to the youth of the day. Tales are told for entertainment value and to share experiences.

Henry Ford said, "Coming together is a

beginning, keeping together is progress, working together is success."

Albert Einstein once said; "When we survey our lives and endeavours, we soon observe that almost the whole of our actions and desires as bound up with the existence of other human beings. We notice that our whole nature resembles that of the social animals.

We eat food that others have produced, wear clothes that others have made, live in houses that others have built. The greater part of our knowledge and beliefs has been communicated to us by other people through the medium of language which others have created. Without language our mental capacities would be poor indeed, comparable to those of the higher animals; we have, therefore, to admit that we owe our principal advantage over the beasts to the fact of living in human society. The individual, if left alone from birth, would remain primitive and beastlike in his thoughts and feelings to a degree that we can hardly conceive."

John Lennon said, 'All you need is love'. The world is as we dream it, and we've been living a dream that combines excessive materialism with a divide-and-conquer, them-versus-us mentality. It is time to act in ways that support a new dream. It is a dream of love – for ourselves, for each other, for nature, and for the planet. It is a dream that tells us to replace the old dream of a death economy with a new dream of a life economy.

3. Economics 101

Everybody is adamant they know how to pick the winner in a horse race. Some people stake money on a horse simply because they like the name of the horse, its number or the colour of the jockey's uniform. Just after staking their money, people are much more confident of their horse's chances of winning than they were immediately before laying down that bet.

Why do they gamble? They gamble for the excitement and the hope of winning money. Most of them lose their money but a few with just blind luck, win.

Gambling is about luck, but betting isn't. Betting is about two things: psychology and information. A punter, who bets, spends all his time gathering information, about the horses' pedigrees, past and recent performances and how the horses have fared on various distances against other horses and how they had performed on different tracks and weather conditions, what they've been doing in training earlier in the week, what feed they have been given, how much the jockey weight when he got

Things You Should Know

up in the morning.

All the information the others can't be bothered with or unable to get or absorb. Then he pools it, works out the odds and watches what the other gamblers do. If the odds are too high, he usually bets on it, whether he thinks it will win or not.

These punters tend to win more often but not every time as their models do not have access to all the relevant data such as the condition of the horses during the race or the mindset of all the bookmakers, horse owners, trainers and jockeys.

The influential minority play a key role for they place pressure on the horse trainers and jockeys to ensure a different outcome than what is expected and gain financially in the process.

Applying economics for the person in the street is like gambling on the horse races, everybody has an opinion and everybody sounds like an authority, and nobody gets it right.

Economists are like the punters they are also gathering relevant data and putting it in their mathematical model. The test is which data to collect, which values should be applied and how to interpret the results. The big question is do they have access to all the relevant data? Models, at best, produce answers consistent with the assumptions put into them.

One of the striking things about the development of modern economics is how long it took for finance to be taken seriously. Stock markets have existed since Roman times, when state-chartered companies carried out many of the functions of the empire such as issuing stocks and bonds. It wasn't till the 1960's that the study of financial markets started to be integrated with the rest of economics. The sheer scale of the financial market problem is breathtaking

The economic life is permeated with uncertainty and that is why people are puzzled about the failure of so many brilliant academic economists to anticipate financial crises. Public officials cannot be expected to be completely candid at all times but should not make misleading statements of any foreseeable crises.

Many leading macro economists and prominent finance theorists simply kept silent as the storm gathered and broke, feeling it was the prudent course to take. Although that is worrying, what is more disturbing is the fact not only were warning signs ignored until it was too late but they did not prepare any contingency plans in how to deal with the financial crisis.

When the stock markets crashed around

the world during 2007/8, the Queen of England visited the London School of Economics to open the New Academic Building. While she was there she listened in on academic lectures. The Queen, who avoids controversy and almost never lets people know what she's thinking, finally asked a simple question about the financial crisis," How was it nobody could foresee it?' No one could answer her.

Although no one answered the Queen's question that day, there were economists who predicted the economic crisis and even wrote about it but they were ignored by the main stream media. Why was that?

As said by Yogi Berra. "In theory there is no difference between theory and practice. In practice there is."

If the real world were accurately described by economic textbooks, there would never have been a financial crisis, the Great Depression would not have happened. The economy would instead be either in equilibrium, or rapidly returning to it, with full employment, low inflation, and sensible priced assets.

Of course, the real world is nothing like that. Instead it has been mostly in disequilibrium, and in near-turmoil and prone to breakdowns as it moves through the cycles.

André Klopper

Although some people find economics technical and boring; but whether we like it or not the impact of the global economy has an effect on all of us, touching our lives in every way. The policies influence the value of our currencies in our pockets, the price of the groceries we buy, how much it cost to fill up our cars, the wages we earn, the interest we get on our savings accounts, and the health of our pension funds.

You may not care about economics but it will have an impact on whether you can retire comfortably, send your children to university, or be able to afford your home.

It is therefore important to study the economic trends and have the knowledge to prepare your portfolio for the next financial cycle. By being innovative with your financial knowledge it will ensure that you stay in the driver's seat.

When we think of a "financial outlook" it is natural to think of macroeconomic variables, such as growth rates, inflation rates, and the manner in which they are connected. But by studying these trends and drivers you will see how the numbers work, and obtain the real value of money matters.

John Law was a Scottish mathematician, gambler and early economist who left his homeland after killing a man in a duel. He found his way to France in the dying days of Louis XIV. By the end of Louis XIV's reign the monarchy was essentially bankrupt. Given the country's debts, the regent was attracted to the ideas of John Law, who persuaded him that the creation of a bank, with the right to issue paper money, was his best option.

Law was the first economist to implement 'money easing' as a way of boosting an economy. He argued that, if his plan was adopted, the people may be employed, the country improved, manufacturing could advance, trade could continue; and wealth and power could be attained.

Gold and silver had previously been thought of as 'real wealth' but Law believed the vital role of money was the oil in the wheel of commerce. "Money is not the value for which goods are exchanged but the value by which they are exchanged" he wrote. "The use of money is to buy goods. Silver, while money is of no other use."

He said they did not have to wait for new gold and silver which was holding trade back but to create more money which would lead to more trade and more wealth. He believed money was in short supply, and more should be created.

The duc d'Orléans, the regent decreed that all taxes and royal revenues could be paid in the notes of Law's bank, the Banque Générale.

Had the scheme been kept on a modest scale, with bank notes backed by gold and silver, French economic growth might indeed have been boosted over the long run. But the regent wanted, and Law promised, quicker results. They created shares in their American exploring company. Due to speculation and prospects of high dividends share prices quickly rose.

While things were going well, Law was the toast of the aristocracy in Paris, as people clamoured to buy shares. While the price was rising few wanted to sell. Law paid the dividends from the money raised in new issues; the definition of a Ponzi scheme. It was one of the great bubbles in history. It could not last. Law tried various schemes to stop the inflationary impact of the extra money he created without also destroying the speculative frenzy that had supported his scheme.

The speculative frenzy was the key to Law's popularity. When the share price of his bank collapsed, he was dismissed from royal service, eventually dying in poverty.

The French developed a suspicion of banks and paper money which lasted into the twentieth century.

Adam Smith, a bookish Scot who was born in Kirkcaldy six months after his father, who was a lawyer, died. Smith studied moral philosophy at Glasgow University and then at Oxford University, before being made Professor at Glasgow University. He supported free markets and opposed business monopolies. He wrote *The Wealth of Nations* in 1776 in which he questioned the wisdom of monarchical rule in the British Empire and his main focus was certain aspects of property rights.

To prevent a recurrence of credit busts he advocated preventing banks from issuing notes to speculative lenders. He based his arguments not on abstract principles but on acute observation.

Smith's view was that it made sense for someone to borrow money if they thought they could earn a higher return than the interest they paid; for example starting a business. It did not make sense to borrow money to finance immediate consumption.

Micro economists were long stuck on the crucial question of what gave a product value until they had a breakthrough in the 1870's with their demand and supply model explaining how the pricing mechanism works in determining the market price.

They mathematically demonstrated a market clearing set of prices. It was the beginning of modern microeconomic theory but was based on an ideal free market system that does not exist.

The next macro-economic breakthrough was the focus on capital, the role of capital and the payment for capital in a modern economy. It gave an understanding of interest payments as compensation for the time value of money and as compensation for the riskiness of an investment.

Modern macroeconomics is an attempt to explain in a more sophisticated way than simple supply and demand theories how economics work. John Maynard Keynes studied how governments funded wars in the past through borrowing money. He broadened the concept to how governments could borrow money to stimulate the economy, or conversely to run a budget surplus to reduce economic activity. Issues surrounding government borrowing and spending are called fiscal policy.

Keynes's theory was that an economy churned because of three basic actions: consumer spending, business spending and government spending. When a recession crept in, and businesses got wiped out and consumers were laid off and unable to spend money then government spending needs to increase to keep the economy afloat and reduce unemployment. Under the Keynesian mixed economy there would still be recessions but would be short-lived. The most important lesson he had learned in the financial markets was that investing and many other economic activities are carried out on the basis of information that is limited and unreliable.

He was a fierce critic of the gold exchange standard of the 1920s, but was practical enough to realise that currencies must be anchored to something and, for this reason, preferred a global commodity standard to the dollar-and-gold standard that emerged from Bretton Woods in 1944.

The gross domestic product (GDP) consist of four basic components namely consumption (C), investment (I), government spending (G) and net exports which is exports (X) minus imports (M). Thus GDP = C + I + G + (X-M)

In theory, business investment could expand on its own, but it makes no sense to invest in plant and equipment beyond a certain point if the customers are not going to buy the resulting goods and services. Therefore in a distressed economy, when consumption (C) is stagnant or declining, investment (I) is tied to it.

According to the Keynes model when the economy is stagnant the government needs to increase their spending to boost the economy.

Friedrich Hayek an Austrian born in

Vienna believed that markets free from democratic intervention could make everyone richer and create an economic utopia. He dismissed collectivist planning as impractical and worked on the causes of business cycles formulating the view that slumps were the inevitable result of prior booms, during which growth had become 'unbalanced', with investment in industrial capacity outstripping the supply of savings in the economy. Recessions, in his view, were a way of restoring the balance between saving and investment.

Milton Friedman who was born in 1912 in Brooklyn, America, was primarily a macroeconomist. He studied how monarchies printed money to finance wars and applied it more broadly to the whole economy as a means of stimulating or reducing overall economic activity. This also led to a much clearer theoretical foundation for the causes of inflation. He wrote *Capitalism and Freedom* and promoted monetary policies.

Neoclassical economics advocated reducing government intervention in the economy and let markets – especially finance markets – decide economic outcomes unimpeded by politicians, bureaucrats or regulations. They believed the only policy tool in favour was manipulation of the interest rate with the objective of controlling the rate of inflation. The flaw in their theory is the issues they ignore that are vital in understanding how a market operates, and their failure to monitor the dynamics of private debt.

More than a century ago Henry George in his book *Progress and Poverty*, sets out to answer a fundamental question of the Gilded Age: Why are so many people living in poverty, while others are getting so rich in an expanding economy?

Today, Piketty's new book –Capital in the Twenty-First Century- is altering the debate about wealth, income and the future of capitalism and is set to be Harvard University Press's all-time best-seller. He proves no more than what we already knew: the rich get richer. He states that there is a flaw in capitalism, an automatic consequence of the dynamic law of accumulation. If we don't fix it, the consequences are "potentially terrifying." He says capitalism should be regulated and that progressive taxation is part of that regulation.

An 80% tax rate on the very high incomes and a graduated scale on personal fortunes from 0.1% for holdings worth around $1.5 million through to 10% for fortunes in the billions of dollars would "contain the unlimited growth of global inequality of wealth."

Piketty's critics dismiss the idea of a globally agreed tax on wealth as unrealistically Utopian, as does Piketty himself.

André Klopper

Empirically tested mathematical models were developed to predict future trends. The models are a good step in the right direction in making economics more scientific. By studying the data obtained from these models economists are able to predict what could happen in the future. There is a small group of economists that knows what is going to happen and write and talk about it. They are all extremely smart, have PhDs from prestigious universities, and are generally decent, honest people trying to do their job well.

However, they have to overcome two obstacles namely; the herding instinct and the pressure from the policy makers.

The herding instinct is quite strong among people, at first they do things according to their own interest but over time they have a tendency to imitate their friends and colleagues. This tendency increases until something breaks it up.

Scharfstein-Stein- "The underlying model idea is that if you do something dumb, but everybody else is doing the same dumb thing at the same time, people won't think of you as stupid, and it won't be harmful to your reputation."

Economists might feel proud about the advances in economic science over the last seven decades since the Great Depression, but that doesn't mean that there has been unanimity about how crises should be handled.

Despite the massive resources spent, the world leading economists still have it wrong. There are three reasons for this. There are some that are pretty happy and their current thinking that no fundamental change is necessary. Others rightly predict what is going to happen but in fear of ridicule or by the pressure from politicians they don't tell people the truth, but rather the 'good news' which the people prefer to hear.

The second reason is the data they are using is wrong because almost all economic data gets revised later. Therefore the real time data which they are using is subject to change. They should use data and prices that are not subject to change which contains reliable clues about the future.

The third reason for being wrong is the same as in betting on horses. The influential minority controls the wealth of the earth, the media and the leading politicians. Their influence distorts the data and makes the mathematical models less reliable.

If economists were merely wrong at betting on horse races, their failure would be harmlessly amusing. But central bankers have the power to create money, change interest rates, and affect our lives in every way-and they don't have a clue.

People who want to know about forecasts are mostly concerned about recessions as it affects the availability of jobs and unemployment during a downturn in economic activity.

Unfortunately, economists are no use to them as they make lousy soothsayers. Economists are unfortunately more philosophers than scientists as they struggle to inform us what happened during the past year, let alone in the year to come.

Economists promised that through fine tuning fiscal and monetary policy, rebalancing terms of trade and spreading risk through derivatives, market fluctuation would be smoothed out and the arc of growth extended beyond what had been possible in the past.

When the world economy went into freefall in 2008, so did our beliefs. The policies of the IMF and the U.S. Treasury had made the crises far worse than they otherwise would have been. The policies showed a lack of understanding of the fundamentals of modern macroeconomics. As a society, we have now lost respect for our long-standing economic gurus.

The panic of 2008 however revealed the economic emperors wore no clothes. Only massive government interventions involving bank capital, interbank lending, money market guarantees, mortgage guarantees, deposit insurance and many other expedients prevented the wholesale collapse of capital markets and the world economy.

Central banks targets inflation and jobs which are both lagging indicators in economy. Lagging indicators can tell you only about the past, not the future. Unemployment is usually at the lowest level just prior to a recession, and inflation is usually the highest in the throes of a recession. Coincident indicators tell you about the present.

To look ahead to what's going on in an economy one must use leading indicators such as building permits, growth in the money supply, average hours worked and the yield curve.

After obtaining a building permit one hires builders who build the house. Once the house is completed you buy appliances and furniture. Building has a huge positive effect on many other parts of the economy. Knowing whether building permits are rising or falling gives you a pretty good advance on where the economy is heading.

The yield curve is the spread between the interest rates on the ten-year Treasury note and the three-month Treasury bill which is found on the back page of *The Economist*. It is simple to use and significantly outperforms other financial and microeconomic indicators. An inversion of the yield curve predicted every recession in the past forty years and since 2012 the yield curve is in a sharp decline.

These leading economic indicators are the most useful, and they are generally ignored by leading economists. Investors who focus on them will find themselves ahead of the game.

However, the central banks are distorting inputs into the economy and leading indicators.

The Global economy is one in which the dynamic process of integration among national economies has succeeded. Business people have to consider a single global economy as part of their decision making. They have to factor in global trends before making any practical decision to invest or not to invest in a venture.

But the world economists focus on their own national economies rather than a single global economy. The absence of a single global economy is because it is at odds with the economist discipline. The key analytical point of international economists is not how a single economy performs, but how many economies deal with each other.

Things You Should Know

The lesson we obtained from studying economics is that there are no easy answers in economics. Fortunately, economic science has not stood entirely still. A new paradigm has emerged in the past twenty years. The new thinking comes with a healthy dose of humility; many practitioners acknowledge the limitations of what is possible with the tools at hand.

They are discovering that complex systems arise spontaneously, behave unpredictably, exhaust resources, and collapse catastrophically.

'Microeconomics concerns things that economists are specifically wrong about, while macroeconomics concerns things economists are wrong about generally." –P.J. O'Rourke, Eat the Rich.

When you are among people who tells you the answer to the current economic problem is to tie their currency to gold, always balance the budget, protect manufacturing and eliminate red tape, walk away as they frankly do not understand much about the running of a modern economy. By walking away, you will not be alone for most academic economists know that macroeconomics consists of complex systems that are extremely difficult to forecast and they are too eager to dismiss forecasting as an activity for fools and frauds. The lesson from all this is: economics is about people and their behaviour.

I believe that if the economists understand the value of demographics they can identify some key economic trends which affect our lives, businesses, and investments during our lifetime. Demographic data can help identify macro and micro trends. One the small side, it will show that people spend the most on potato chips at the age of forty-two, and deflation can set in when more people retire than enter the workforce.

Economists think no one can predict longer-term trends because the world and technologies are changing faster than ever. The truth is we have new information on demographics that we never had before, which makes predicting the long-term economic trends easier than predicting shorter term trends. It is the best leading indicator as people do predictable things as they age.

Demographics show that young people cause inflation as they cost everything and produce nothing. As the new generation enters the workforce, businesses have to invest in workspace, equipment, and training. Conversely, older people tend to be more deflationary. They spend less, downsize in major durable goods, borrow less, and save more. They don't require investments in new infrastructure like offices or larger homes, or in more education; they ultimate leave the workforce and downsize to smaller homes or even nursing homes. This stands in contrast to young people who require massive investments in education, office space and technology as they prepare for and then enter the workforce.

4. Banking

Trade in the seventeenth century Europe was conducted primarily with gold and silver coins. Coins were durable and had value in themselves, but they were hard to transport in bulk and could be stolen if not kept under lock and key.

Many people therefore deposited their coins with the goldsmiths who had the strongest safes in town. The goldsmiths issued convenient paper receipts that could be traded in place of the bulkier coins they represented.

Receipts were much lighter, safer and easier to carry. These receipts were also used when people who needed the coins came to the goldsmiths for loans.

The goldsmiths realised that between 10% and 20% of their receipts came back to be redeemed in gold at any one time. Therefore they began creating 'paper money' worth five times the gold they actually held and with this they increased interest and became very wealthy.

The system was called 'fractional reserve" banking as the gold held in reserve was a mere fraction of the banknotes it supported.

This created a problem that almost all money comes from banker created loans and the only way to get the interest owned on old loans is to take out new loans, continually inflating the money supply; either that or some borrowers have to default.

Since money was invented people were exposing moneylenders and people in power, for their extravagances and causing misery amongst the people. Sometimes they misunderstood what they denounced.

For the rich financiers to keep workers on the treadmill they must create enough new debt-money to cover the interest on their loans. If they create too much they would dilute the value of their own money.

The idea of public finance began with the sea battle between the Anglo-Dutch fleet and the French fleet. Under orders of the British Queen in 1690 the Allied fleet attacked the French fleet. The allied fleet was crushed and the naval defeat shook England to the core.

England needed funds for re-armament and in 1694 the state created the Bank of England to raise money. Private subscribers to the

Bank's capital raised £1.2 million in twelve days.

All that money was lent to the King, and half was immediately used to rebuild the Royal Navy. It was money well spent as the English enjoyed for almost two centuries naval dominance. That is why countries have debt.

During the war of Independence, The Civil War, World War One, Pearl Harbour and World War Two, America had to take on debt as they saw it as the price of liberty. In ordinary times the government should not take on further debt but repay their debt. It would be a wise decision to save during peace time for any emergencies.

The War of Independence (30% of GDP) was paid off in 1835. For each war since they borrowed money and soon after the wars ended began to repay the debt. The only time the U.S. did borrow money without a war up to 1980, was during the Great Depression.

Fundamentals of borrowing and lending;

(i) A person borrows money to buy things such as a house, car, etc. is increasing his present consumption at the expense of his future consumption.

(ii) People and companies borrow money in order to produce things, they are increasing their present production and increasing current economic activity.

(iii) A person that saves or invests is reducing his current consumption in order to increase his future consumption.

Economists like to call the banking system the heart of the economy; it pumps money to the places where it is needed most. Banking serves a public utility function, and the question government regulators must wrestle with is how far private financiers should be allowed to seek a profit and to what degree they must be required to ensure that money flows safely.

If banks over extended their assets, failing to keep adequate reserve capital to cover potential losses, they are at risk of collapse.

'Money, being naturally barren to make it breed money is preposterous and perversion from the end of its institution, which was only to serve the purpose of exchange and not of increase...Men called bankers we shall hate, for they enrich themselves while doing nothing.' – Aristotle, Politics

"Capital must protect itself in every possible way, both by combination and legislation. Debts must be collected, mortgages foreclosed as rapidly as possible. When, through process of law, the common people lose their homes, they will become more docile and more easily governed through the strong arm of government applied by a central power of wealth under leading financiers. These truths are well known among our principal men, who are now engaged in forming an imperialism to govern the world. By dividing the voters through the political party system, we can get them to expend their energies in fighting for questions of no importance. It is thus, by discrete action, we can ensure for ourselves that which has been so well planned and so successfully accomplished." –Montagu Norman, Governor of the Bank of England, addressing the United States Bankers' Association, New York, 1924.

Prior to the crash of 2007-8 banks were taking bigger and bigger risks, lending more, investing more, because assets had been rising in value for years, and fewer and fewer borrowers were reneging on their debts.

Since the 1980's the banks had a second source of false corroboration for they believed they were no longer prone to normal downturns. They were all using new complicated financial models-run by computers- called Value at Risk models, to assist how much they can lose at any instant if there were a sudden fall or rise in markets.

The problem with this model was that the data captured movements in markets that had taken place the previous ten years or so, when things were pretty stable. The models for minimising risk were built on the assumption that the very worst that had happened in the past would not and could not happen again.

The more data was fed into these models the more unlikely it showed that big swings might happen and the consequences of that had encouraged bankers to take even bigger risks.

Bankers and investors became more and more irrationally exuberant and certain that a new golden age of ever-rising prosperity had arrived. They magnified the debt of the consuming countries like the U.S. and UK, by lending more and more to households, to businesses and to governments.

With the banking system at the brink of collapse in the fall of 2008, lending dried up and the U.S. government stepped in to bail out the bankers and their shareholders who caused the problems. Instead of developing a more efficient and accountable financial system the bankers walked away with trillions of dollars. Bank executives acted in their own self-interest by getting as much money for themselves and their shareholders as they could.

The banking world was shaken by another major scandal in 2014. It included Barclays, Citygroup, JPMorgan chase and the Royal Bank of Scotland who pleaded guilty to rigging the price of foreign currencies and were fined more than $2.5 billion. Within a year these four banks, plus one other UBS, would be fined an additional $1.6 billion, along with another $1.3 billion in the case of Barclays, to settle related claims. Since 2007, the banks had operated as 'cartels' and the US Attorney General Loretta Lynch described their behaviour as 'a brazen display of collusion and foreign exchange rate manipulation'.

Real reforms are needed as the financial system had grown out of proportions while exploiting those who don't have the financial know how. The whole banking system should be put into receivership and the bankers should be jailed as fraudsters.

5. The Consumer Exploitation

Despite going without the latest fashion items we still manage to go through a bewildering amount of money every month. The cost of living is sky-rocketing despite the government's attempts to persuade us to the contrary. Every part of our lives have been hijacked and robbed of its real value by financial transactions that hurts our purse and empties our soul.

André Klopper

Merchandising and marketing have been systematically employed to drive consumption up to ever-higher levels until it will have huge ramifications for everyone. Our population is bombarded by advertising, marketing and merchandising in order to promote capitalism, if people have enough they must be persuaded to want more. It became the norm that children demand the latest electronic equipment and a new car when they are old enough to obtain their drivers licence.

Advertising has become such a big part of our culture, we are mostly unaware of the ways it influences our desires, the ways we spend our money, and to what extent we're willing to legally obligate money we haven't earned yet. Simply put, advertising is the art of convincing people to spend money they do or do not have for something they do not need.

Two particularly destructive forms of marketing are planned obsolescence and throw away products- the creation of products that are deliberately designed to have short lives and thus force "over consumption." This technique was brought to perfection in the mid-twentieth century by the automobile industry, which introduced superficially changed models every year.

The automobile industry's success was copied by almost every other corporation. Noted product designer Brooks Stevens explained why in a 1958 interview: Our whole economy is based on planned obsolescence and everybody who can read without moving their lips should know it by now. We make good products, we induce people to buy them, and then next year we deliberate introduce something that will make those products old fashioned, out of date, obsolete. We do that for the soundest reason: to make money.

In recent decades electronic industries have become masters of planned obsolescence, designing and selling products that can't be upgraded or repaired and that are replaced by new models within months of introduction.

The most extreme form of planned obsolescence is the throw away product; it's been estimated that 80 percent of all products sold in the United States are designed to be used once and then throw away. The most egregious example is packaging, which has been called "garbage waiting to happen."

Advertisers rely on marketing theory that states people are driven by four things: fear, guilt, greed and the need for approval.

The human spirit and the environment are progressively sacrificed upon the altar of unrestrained greed. Not only do we worship our materialism money god but we've accepted it as our saviour. Despite urgent messages from reality to the contrary, conventional wisdom persists in reinforcing the beliefs that money will make us happy, weaponry will make us safe, drugs will make us healthy, and more and more information will make us wise.

Turnover is increased by the advertising of huge savings for customers during their sales campaigns. Customers buying during these shopping sprees are convinced they are making large saving by buying items at reduced prices but they are only spending, saving absolutely nothing. Volume discounts are cleverly marketed as loyalty rewards getting the customers to consume even more.

The truth is that the more we shop the more we own, the more chores, hassles and complications we create in our lives. There is certainly no more time left for quiet contemplation, idle dreaming or even anything resembling careful thinking.

People are bombarded over the radio and TV with one hard and fast rule: spending more money is good, and spending less money is bad for the country. Shopping is good. Reducing debt is bad for the country.

This is completely wrong. If people are spending money they don't have, that may be good in the short term for the stores and manufactures, but it's often bad in the long term for the whole economy.

Things You Should Know

Borrowing money to invest in might be alright but going into debt for consumption is generally not the right thing to do.

Companies are experiencing rising costs at the real inflation rate which is higher than what the governments wish to admit. They don't want to raise prices in line with costs without alienating their customers. So what do they do? Perhaps they give customers a little less for their money, or they put something less substantial in their products and hope no-one will notice.

Studies have proved that the conflict between cost increases and limited pricing power is leading to the use of cheaper ingredients and deceptive packaging across the economy. Trusted brands, in short, are becoming untrustworthy.

Why don't people notice this? This is because people are lemming their way to oblivion, entertained every step of the way by mindless gadgetry and endless diversions.

The theory of consumer sovereignty rests on the assumption that consumers know everything about the products they want to buy, and as such make informed and rational buying decisions. This is a fallacy.

Every part of the capitalist system is characterised by 'information asymmetry'-the sellers have far more information than the buyers. Although economists rarely admit this, sellers routinely conceal important information from buyers.

Frederick Robbins, an early researcher for the contraceptive pill, argued that the potentially harmful population control methods served a greater good. Malcolm Potts, medical director of the IPPF, dismissed safety concerns about the contraceptive drug Depo-Provera. "We are not going to know whether Depo-Provera is safe, until a large number of women use it for a very long time...You cannot prove a drug is safe until you use it." While Depo-Provera was given to millions of women in the third world, it was banned in the United States.

The main drivers for the release of Depo-Provera were corporate profits and reduced population growth in the third world countries.

A hundred and fifty years ago the average working class women in Britain was lucky if she owned her own hairbrush and a pair of copper cooking pots. Women and children often lived on little more than potatoes, bread and butter. The average man's most valued possessions were an inherited pocket watch and a couple of starched collars.

At the beginning of the 20th century things began to change with mass production, distribution, marketing and promotion. The speed with which the products infiltrated and moulded people's lives was astonishing. The middle class was created on an ever increasing speeding merry-go round of production and consumption that is now out of control. Having more and newer things each year has become not just something we want but something we need.

How many people are poor these days? People questioned the standard of poverty as people with incomes less than 60% of the national median, when 30 years ago that same amount would have been a fortune.

Our basic needs as humans are few: shelter, food, and clothing. Everything else is a "want". Distinguishing a need from a want is not quite that easy. Living in a country where there is so much abundance and so many choices, a sense of entitlement can muddy the waters when it comes to what we want and what we need. Most people have an elevated sense of entitlement simply because they have no idea how fortunate they are.

We have past the point that we need any more but the nature of human desire means that however much we have, we will always want more. The cult of consumption has lured us into the belief that buying lots of lovely things will make us happy. Without these things not only our lives but also ourselves, and our personality would be lacking.

André Klopper

The rapid growing self-storage industry in the developed world bears testimony to the fact that we have become so addicted to stuff and a materialistic way of life, with serious difficulty distinguishing between needs and wants. Every month millions of households are paying a public storage facility to store the stuff they deserve and just could not live without. Almost one in ten households in the developed world now rents a unit in which to cram a whole lot of stuff they never use.

Between 1950 and 1993 the average size of a new house built in the United States increased by nearly 90 percent (1,100 versus 2060 square feet) while the average household size decreased.

In 1973, sixty percent of new homes had more than two bathrooms and by 2005, ninety-five percent of new homes had two or more bathrooms, and 26 percent had three or more bathrooms. Note that 40 percent of the world's population does not have indoor plumbing.

Since the 1950's the average size of a kitchen in a new American home has more than tripled, to approximate 285 square feet. Who is cooking in those big new kitchens? Between 1980 and 2000, the frequency of purchasing meals outside the home (restaurants and takeaways) more than doubled, to more than 30 percent of all the meals they eat. In fact 19 percent of all meals eaten by adults in America are now consumed in their cars.

6. The Evolution of Money

Money: the word itself comes from a title of the Roman deity Juno Moneta- the goddess of warning and advice; a suitable omen for those who rely too much on its value.

The idea of paper money has been around for more than a thousand years, having been introduced by the Chinese. The Emperor Hein Tsung, who ruled from 806 to 821, used paper currency to overcome a copper shortage. The concept was then developed by the Mongols who took over the Chinese Empire. Marco Polo describes how the Grand Khan of the Mongols used paper money. He was surprised why people accept paper money as payment as it has no intrinsic value.

The answer was that the traders had little choice. The value of the paper money was equivalent to the citizens' belief in the stability of the governing regime. The rule of the Mongols did not last for ever and nor did the value of the currency. The temptation to print more money was simply too great. According to economist Roger Bootle, the supply of paper money increased sixfold between 1190 and

1240, while prices raised twenty fold over the same period. By 1448, notes nominally worth one thousand in cash were actually trading for three. That was one of the last historical references to Chinese paper money. The nation switched to silver, a system that lasted into the twentieth century.

Money itself has no utility but functions as a means of exchange, a store of value and a unit of account. Money is valuable only insofar as you can trade it for something else of value. It is far more useful than precious metals as it is far easier to use to clear a vast spider's web of transactions between global banks, companies and consumers if they are all entries on a computer, than it is to transport bullion over vast distances.

Money evolved as human society grew more sophisticated and required a more sophisticated means of doing business. Money is the lifeblood of the economy, and unless it circulates readily, the essential economic activities go into the equivalent of cardiac arrest.

When we read about the Fed creating another $800 billion dollars we tend to conjure up images of government printers printing this mountain of money and we try to determine how much inflation this is going to create. We immediately realise that we do not have the necessary data to calculate the inflation and we forget about the whole incident and get on with our lives.

The Fed usually creates money by writing a check for government bonds. These bonds are sold in the open market to banks and other institutions. The banks are allowed to issue newly created banknotes which is called the monetary base. The banks lend some money to the Treasury to pay for ever-expanding government.

It is only when the money is converted into loans and the cash ends up in people's pockets, when the money becomes liquid. Central banks cannot create money without the help of the banking system and the borrowers.

When the speed in which money circulates falls and banks don't increase their lending, it becomes difficult to get money into consumer's hands to stimulate the economy. Therefore when central banks create money which does not circulate, all they do is increase the monetary base while the velocity of money decreases.

If velocity were to keep falling, the central banks could create an almost infinite amount of money and inflation would not rise but real estate, bonds and stock would rise in price. However, the higher the monetary base, the higher potential for inflation.

When central banks buy up all of the

government bonds, it creates problems for the banking system as their funds would be restricted, reducing their collateral to fund loans for new customers.

When interest rates are rising, velocity tends to be high which creates inflation.

One of the first monetary systems was barter. Barter is simply trading a product or a service for another product or service. Barter is fine for a society where only a few things are made and exchanged. But it becomes hopelessly time-consuming as societies grow more complex. The other problems with barter are that it is slow, tedious and hard to measure relative values.

A farmer would trade a sheep for a sack of corn but when they barter in a number of different commodities it became a very inconvenient process. What if the other person wants cows instead of sheep? Then a third person had to get involved. Money made these transactions a lot easier as the sheep, corn, cattle all have a value in monetary terms. A farmer no longer needs to arrange a direct swap as he can sell his livestock or crop for money.

If we are forced back onto the barter system it will be hard for the government to tax barter transactions as the tax department does not accept chickens.

To speed up the process of exchange, groups of people came to agree on tangible items that represented value. Seashells were some of the first forms of commodity money. So were stones, coloured gems, beads, cattle, goats, gold and silver. The use of commodities sped up the process of exchange and more business could be done in less time.

The split tally was used in medieval Europe, which was constantly short of money. In order to record bilateral exchange and debts square sticks were marked with a system of notches and then split lengthwise. This way the two halves both recorded the same notches and each party to the transaction received one half of the marked stick as proof.

Later this technique was refined in various ways and become virtually tamper proof. One of the refinements was to make the two halves of the stick different lengths.

The longer part was called stock and was given to the party which had advance the money to the receiver. The shorter part was called the foil. The split tally was accepted as legal proof in medieval courts.

The idea of paper money had been re-introduced in 1650 in a pamphlet titled "The Key to Wealth" and was based on the receipts issued by the goldsmiths. With the colonies using foreign coins to conduct trade they were always short of coins as they imported more than they exported. This caused the colonies to be without enough money for their own internal needs.

The Massachusetts Assembly proposed a new kind of money, a "bill of credit" representing the governments I.O.U. - it promise to pay tomorrow on a debt incurred today. Other colonies followed suit with their own issues of paper money.

Benjamin Franklin, an enthusiast for paper money said "The riches of a country are to be valued by the quantity of labour its inhabitants are able to purchase and not by the quantity of the gold and silver they possess."

When gold was the medium of exchange, money determined production rather than production determining the money supply. When gold was plentiful, things got produced.

When it was scarce, men were out of work and people knew wants. The virtue of government-issue money was, it underwrote production of goods and services that would not otherwise have been on the market, thus creating real wealth.

The first credit card was introduced in 1951, and shopping became a national sport. With the advent of the suburbs, shopping centres sprang up like weeds.

Since then money in all its forms are used more and more to smooth out transactions between different individuals, groups and nations. It is a way of storing and exchanging value, of making and recording promises. Banks are used to facilitate these processes and overall it is working very well.

People have placed their trust in their currency by which all values are measured, by which social status is guaranteed, upon which security depends, and in which the fruits of labour is stored. It freed us from old constraints that kept people poor, sick and short-lived. It brought wonders that people of the past could not have imagined.

The currency in your hand is not automatically money because it was issued through the Reserve Bank – it's only money if it keeps a reasonable stable value.

Many people will dedicate more time and effort in researching the value and functions of their next electronic device than in their long term savings plan. Managing money is a dedicated task since you worked hard to build your nest egg and therefore you should have proper time devoted in managing it. Determine your objectives, know your risk tolerance, and develop a discipline investment plan and strategy. Remember that there is some luck involved in investing but it also comes with a risk.

As it is your money have a properly constructed portfolio that meets your objective.

Money mistakes

1. Not having a plan, or having one that won't work.
2. Having goals that are too general.
3. Lack of spending/savings/investment discipline.
4. Procrastinating about financial decisions.
5. Making decisions based on emotion (fear and greed).
6. Too impatient, wanting instant success.
7. No medium or long term plans.
8. Speculation instead of investing.
9. Being too conservative or aggressive.
10. Being overly influenced by others (friends and family).

Why should we care about money?

1. Because money is important. Its impact is also emotional, spiritual and personal.

2. Because money impact our lives. It determines where we live, what we drive, where our kids go to school. It is the means by which we pay our bills, protect our families, and prepare for the future. Wrong choices and bad decisions can turn an otherwise pleasant life into a miserable existence.

3. Because families are finding themselves more financially challenged as prices soar but salaries remain stagnant

4. Because you handle a significant amount of money during your life time.

7. The Gold Standard

Gold has a high density; uniform of grade, does not rust or tarnish and is practically impossible to destroy, except with special acids or explosives. It is malleable and therefore easily shaped into coins and bars. Finally it has a longer track record as money; over eight thousand years.

Gold is not a commodity, nor is it an investment but is money par excellence.

Given these properties of scarcity, durability, uniformity the case for gold as money seems strong. Yet modern central bankers and economists do not take gold seriously as a form of money.

"I next argued that the gold standard, the fixing of rates of exchange and so forth were shibboleths which I have never regarded and never would regard as weighty and immutable principles of economy. Money to me, was simply a token of exchange for work done, and its value depended absolutely on the value of the work accomplished. Where money did not represent services rendered, I insisted it had no value at all." – Adolf Hitler.

Gold has served as an international currency since the sixth century BC in Lydia which is modern-day Turkey. England established a gold-backed paper currency at a fixed exchange rate in 1717, which continued in various forms with periodic wartime suspensions until 1931.

Britain adopted the gold standard in 1816, very much against the advice of David Ricardo. By 1914 the gold standard was nearly universal. Although a good deal of gold was used in jewellery the main holders of gold were the world's central banks. The outbreak of the First World War created a need for a huge and inflationary spending on weapons and men the gold standard had to abandon and the printing press churned out money.

Since 1931 most countries used the gold standard for their transactions in the booming world trade market. This meant transactions no longer had to be done with heavy gold bullion or coins. It also increased the trust that was needed for a successful global trade since paper currency now had guaranteed value tied to something real.

The countries adopted the gold standard because it guaranteed that any amount of paper money could be redeemed by the government for its value in gold which has kept their real value over the centuries. Creditors and traders could be sure of the value of money which encouraged them to lend and to trade.

The advantage of the gold standard is that money is backed by a fixed asset. This provides a self-regulating and stabilising effect on the economy as the government can only print as much money as its country has in gold. The stable supply of money discouraged inflation, which is too much money chasing too few goods.

However, as a means of exchange, gold is less suitable: gold's very scarcity makes it impractical as a monetary unit for day to day use. The supply of gold and silver has no relationship at all with economic activity.

In an ideal world, you want the supply of money to grow in line with the economy, gold and silver alone won't do. It is no coincidence that gold and silver fell steadily out of use in the twentieth century, an era when economic growth accelerated rapidly.

Lincoln's economic advisor, Henry Carey believed that America's industrial development was held back by a policy imposed by foreign financiers. He considered 'free trade' and the 'gold standard' as twin financial weapons forged by England for its own economic conquest. His solution to the gold drain was for the government to create an independent national currency that was non-exportable.

The crisis was resolved by President Lincoln who issued "Greenbacks" to make up the budget shortfall and foil the bankers. These notes did not accrue interest and did not have to be paid back to the banks. The "Greenbacks" were halted after Lincoln's assassination.

Even in the early days the gold standard was questioned. In 1863, Eleazar Lord, a New York banker said the requirements that paper banknotes be backed by a certain weight of gold bullion was a fiction. Gold was controlled by the financiers who held the world to ransom. Banks did not have nearly enough gold to "redeem" all the paper money therefore there is no real reason for paper money to be linked to gold.

Since negative trade balances were settled in gold, gold followed the balance of trade. This kept the developing countries which supplied the raw materials in debt as they imported the more expensive finished goods. When gold left the country the banknotes had to be withdrawn from the circulation which caused depression.

The disadvantage of the gold standard caused countries to become obsessed with keeping their gold, rather than improving the business climate. Government actions to protect their gold cause large fluctuations in the economy. Between 1890 and 1905 when the U.S. was on the gold standard, the economy suffered five major recessions for this reason.

During the 1890's America was plagued by an economic depression that was nearly as severe as the Great depression of the 1930s. The American people had been deluded into a belief in scarcity by defining their wealth in terms of a scarce commodity, gold.

There was not enough gold available to finance the needs of an expanding economy. The result was insufficient money and the bankers raised the interest rates. The farmers lived like serfs to the bankers, having mortgaged their farms to the hilt, and they were also exploited by the railway cartel for shipping their products. The factory workers in the cities were no better off as unemployment reached 20%, crime rate soared, families were torn apart and racial tensions boiled.

Before the Federal Reserve could stabilise the gold and currency values World War 1 broke out and European countries suspended the gold standard to print enough money to pay for their military involvement. This caused hyperinflation and the countries realised the value of a gold standard when they returned to a modified gold standard.

After the war Germany frantically search for other means to support their currency, ended up with the Rentenmark. The USA maintained a gold-convertible dollar standard and when Roosevelt fixed the price at $35 per ounce of gold. This became the basis of the Bretton Woods system with all other currencies at fixed rates measured against the dollar, which in turn was valued against the gold. The Bretton Woods system ensured that the US dollar became the international reserve currency in the world which benefited America tremendously.

Every major currency left the gold standard during the Great Depression. Great Britain was the first to do so. Japan and the Scandinavian countries followed suit. The run on American gold forced the country to follow their example in 1933. France, Poland, Belgium and Switzerland stayed on the gold standard until 1936.

For a hundred years the gold standard pegged the price of gold at $20.67 per ounce until Roosevelt increased the gold price to $35 per ounce. He funded the government projects to provide work for the unemployed with borrowed money, indebting the country to a banking cartel, instead of the government just printing the money themselves.

The countries which left the gold standard first also recovered first. China, which had a silver standard, almost avoided the depression entirely. However, when the U.S. with their silver purchase act created an intolerable demand on China's silver coins, they had to abandon their silver standard in 1935 in favour of Chinese 'legal notes'.

The outbreak of World War II ended the Depression, allowing countries to go back on a modified gold standard. Most of these countries adapted the Bretton-Woods System, which set the exchange value for all currencies in terms of gold.

It obligated member countries to convert foreign official holdings of their currencies into gold at these par values.

However, since the U.S. held most of the world's gold; many countries simply pegged the value of their currency to the dollar, making the dollar the 'de facto' world currency.

The Bretton Woods agreement meant central banks had to maintain fixed exchange rates between their currencies and the dollar. This was done by buying their own country's currency in foreign exchange markets if their currency declined against the dollar.

If it became too high, they'd print more of their currency and sell it. As the countries no longer needed to exchange their currency for gold as the dollar had replaced it, and the dollar increased in value.

During the 1960's as the U.S economy prospered, consumers imported more and paid in dollars. This large balance of payment deficit concerned foreign governments that the U.S. could no longer back up the dollar in gold.

In the late 1960's President Charles de Gaulle of France challenged the hegemony of the dollar in the world's money markets by pushing as much as possible of the French monetary reserves out of the US dollar and into gold. He and his monetary advisor, Jacques Rueff believed in the role of gold as a permanent store of value although this view had long been ridiculed by Keynesians. Charles de Gaulle and Rueff believed that the price of gold was being artificially held down by the political fact of dollar dominance and his aim was to force a large-scale devaluation of the dollar against the gold. This move was naturally resisted strongly by the US Treasury. There were even a few assassination attempts on de Gaulle's life during this period.

Gold had enough followers in every country in the world to make a difference and as de Gaulle and the gold followers bought more and more gold the Americans were increasingly embarrassed by having to sell their ingots at the prevailing price of $35 per ounce. Many other European countries had followed in France's wake and quietly accumulated large gold reserves. This led to a sharp reduction in American's gold reserves.

The American power was being battered through the 1960s both by Vietcong in Vietnam and by the French offensive in the gold market.

In 1950 the United States had official gold reserves of over 20,000 metric tons but due to persistent large trade deficits their gold reserves dropped to just over 9,000 metric tonnes when Nixon pulled the plug on gold. Britain's gold reserves dropped from 2,500 metric tonnes to only 690 metric tonnes over the same period while Germany, France, Italy and the Netherlands increased their gold reserves by almost 11,000 metric tonnes.

By 1970, the U.S only held $14.5 billion in gold against foreign holdings of $45.7 billion. In 1971 President Nixon increased the price of gold to $38 per ounce and the Fed stopped redeeming dollars with gold.

The system finally broke down in the 1970's with the adoption of a floating exchange rate by the USA in 1973, an example followed by the rest of the developed world. Gold was no longer exchangeable against the dollar and lost its place within the system. The gold price was now free to oscillate like that of any other metal and it moved up sharply from $35 to nearly $200 in a matter of months. De Gaulle's policy was richly rewarded when the gold price soared after 1973 and the French reserves were multiplied almost six-fold in value.

The resulting situation is peculiar. Gold had no place in the world's monetary system but the world's central banks still hold gold reserves. They did this as they believed that gold have an insurance value – that is, its value tends to rise in times of crisis – and the fact the rising price of gold meant that many countries saw their reserves increased markedly in value.

Once the gold standard was dropped, countries began printing more of their own currency. Inflation usually resulted, but for the most abandoning the gold standard created more economic growth.

America tried to keep a downward pressure on the gold price because a weak dollar means a higher gold price and vice versa. They believed that if the world retains confidence in the dollar as the world's international reserve currency, then there should be no perceive flight into gold. Thus despite the fact that gold is notionally irrelevant to the world's monetary system, in practice it continues to play a shadow role and each new challenger in turn to American power tends to express that challenge through upward pressure on the gold price.

The world placed an anti-apartheid trade boycott on South Africa which left the country in a parlous position and their only way out was a higher gold price as they produced three quarters of the world's gold. Gold soared to over $800 per ounce which led to South Africa's growth in their economy while the rest of the world slumped into recession after the 1973 oil crisis.

When Kissinger wished to provide President Ford with a diplomatic success before the 1976 November election he was determined to push South Africa's premier, John Voster to pressure Ian Smith for majority rule in Rhodesia.

The US therefore exerted heavy downward pressure on the gold price and South Africa through staging IMF and US treasury gold sales to cash in on gold's high value but also to increase the value of the American dollar. This caused other countries to sell off some of their gold holdings to save their currencies. The result was that by the 1990s gold had fallen back to as low as $250 per ounce.

As concern grew that the un-coordinated sales of gold by many central banks were causing the value of gold reserves to fall for everyone. This necessitated the European central banks to sign the Washington Agreement on Gold (CBGA1). Under this agreement gold sales were not to exceed a total of 400 tonnes per year.

This stabilised the gold price until the

world financial crisis of 2008-09 led to widespread panic and suddenly central banks not only ceased to sell gold but turned around and began to buy it again in large quantities particular the BRIC nations.

Gold has never lost its appeal as an asset of real value. Whenever recessions or inflation looms, investors return to gold. It reached its record high of $1,895 an ounce on September 5, 2011.

The price of gold is most closely tied to the change in real interest rates. When inflation is above the interest rate that you can get on the cash in your bank account, gold goes up. When inflation is below the level of interest you can earn for your cash, gold will go down.

The price of gold is always anchored to what is agreed on at 10:30 a.m. and 3:00 p.m. every trading day in London by the five banks that belong to the London Gold Market Fixing Ltd. At those times, officers from Barclays Capital, Deutsche Bank, HSBC, Société Générale, and the Bank of Nova Scotia confer to decide upon a price based on how intraday demand and supply factors have functioned until then.

Although gold prices changes throughout the day, the London fix is the one against which all physical transactions are referenced. The simplicity of the London fix fosters a sense of order and confidence in the market.

Western central banks don't allow independent inspection of their vaults or adhere to generally accepted accounting principles. For the last decades they have used their gold to loan it to large bullion banks to sell the gold on the open market.

The gold they've dumped on the market has depressed the metal's exchange rate, making the fiat currency appear relatively stable by masking its eroded value. Gold is made to appear relatively volatile because of short-term fluctuations, while its ability to preserve purchasing power over long periods of time is largely overlooked.

The central banks lump their physical gold and gold loans into one line on their financial reports, lumping tangible gold asset with financial assets with counterparty risk. This accounting deception has enabled central banks to hide the extent to which they've been emptying their gold vaults. In effect, the bullion banks are "short" gold, a liability that is neither reported to the public nor widely understood by bank shareholders.

Analysts working with the Gold Anti-Trust Action Committee and other interested parties have pieced together what they believe is an accurate account of central bank lending, and have concluded that nearly half of the world's official gold reserves of 29,000 tonnes have been dumped on the market this way. So the major fiat currencies actually have even less potential gold backing than previously thought.

In January 2013, the German Bundesbank announced that they wanted about 300 tonnes of the gold stored in the New York Fed's vault returned to Germany. The New York Fed claiming to hold 6,200 tonnes told the Bundesbank that the transfer would take seven years.

In March 2013 the Dutch bank ABN Amro informed customers who had stored gold bullion in its vaults that they could no longer have their gold on demand, in effect defaulting on the storage agreement.

In April 2013 a gold analyst reported that the Swiss central bank had banned the withdrawal of gold from Swiss commercial banks.

Gold inventories at the Comex began to fall rapidly leading to speculation that it might be unable to deliver gold owed to holders of "long" future contracts, and would default by settling in cash rather than metal.

Gold held by exchange-traded funds worldwide began to decline.

Chinese gold imports began to soar, implying that the West where gold was generally perceived to be an investment and out of favour, was shipping large amounts of gold to the East, where buyers saw it as both money and undervalued at prevailing exchange rates.

8. Capitalism

The term 'capital' has two quite different meanings in economics: a sum of money, and a collection of machinery. Economists hoped that the rate of profit would fall smoothly as the amount of capital used in production rose, so that capital, like labour would manifest diminishing marginal productivity. But there is no uniform relationship between the rate of profit and the amount of capital.

The distribution of income between wages and profits is largely independent of the system of production. The distribution of income is a social phenomenon and the economists are fighting against this conclusion.

Just to add to the confusion, Marx saw the difference between the value embodied in a worker and the value the worker added to the production as surplus value or sole source of profit. He also stated that no machine or raw product under any circumstances added more value than their purchased value to the output.

If this was true capital-intensive industries would move into labour intensive industries to improve their profits. The opposite however is considered true.

Capital is resources used to produce goods and services. Capitalism is an economic system in which trade, industry and the means of production are controlled by private owners with the goal of making profits in a market economy. It usually involves the advancing of money today in return for the promise of money in the future.

The Communist system demonstrated what happens when governments replace market price signals with central planning and prices that are administratively determined. As a method of ramping up production of basic goods, such as steel and wheat, collectivism proved pretty effective. But once Communist economics moved beyond the stage of industrialisation, they couldn't deal with the variegated demands of consumer-driven society. Innovation was lacking, and information about consumer preferences got lost, or was ignored.

The five kinds of capitalism;

1) Laissez-faire economics free from government

restrictions with only regulations to protect property rights.

2) Welfare economics include comprehensive social welfare policies.

3) State capitalism is described in which the commercial activity is undertaken by the state.

4) Crony capitalism is a state of affairs in which insider corruption, nepotism and cartels dominate the system.

5) Marxian economics is considered the mature state of capitalism.

In the early days experts generally believed that capitalistic economies gravitate to a natural equilibrium of full employment. Therefore, the government's role in the economy was to do as little as possible.

Will capitalism survive the current depression as it did all the previous depressions? It might survive because there is no alternative that hasn't been thoroughly discredited yet. The alternatives to capitalism are unappealing, to the super rich.

For capitalism to survive in the market place it must grow, compelling producers to find more markets for their growing output. Growth is driven even further by corporate greed to increase their profits. The race to accumulate, the real meaning of economic growth under the system, is endless.

Under capitalism, the only measure of success is how much profit is made every day, every week, every year. It doesn't matter if the profit comes from selling products that are directly harmful to both humans and nature. It does not matter whether it's spreading diseases, destroying forests or polluting the air or water supplies, all that counts is profits.

Most capitalists are working in their own short-term interest and are using raw materials such as metals, minerals, oil and coal as if there is an infinite supply while poisoning the environment to make it inhabitable. In short, pollution and waste are not accidents and are not market failures but the way capitalism operates.

If you ask any top manager or shareholders who control corporations if they want their children and grandchildren to live in a stable and sustainable world, their answer is always a responding yes. But why do their actions contradict their words? Why do they seem determined to leave their children and grandchildren a world of poisoned air and water, a world of floods and droughts and escalating climate disasters?

In the capitalist system cash markets are

markets where people can trade in shares, bonds and commodities. Connected to these cash markets are vast futures, options and other derivatives markets: the futures markets are where you can bet on the future price of a currency, or bond, or commodity; the options markets are where you can buy an 'option' to buy or sell some kind of asset at a future date and at a specified price and the derivatives markets are the generic name for any kind of fancy market.

In risky business such as grain and oil the producers can reduce their risk by selling their products today at a specified price for future delivery. As they are confident of the revenues they will be receiving within in a few months, they can organise their spending in line with the money that will be coming in.

The problem is that once a market of this sort has been established, it tends to attract the great global herd of professional gamblers: banks' dealing desks, hedge funds, wealthy individual speculators and so on. The sheer complexity of the derivative market magnified the riskiness of the financial economy.

The riskiness of all financial trading can be magnified by leverage. When a hedge fund or other speculator buys a derivative they usually only have to put up a fraction of the money needed. Betting on margin, betting with borrowed money, means speculators can put on more and bigger bets with limited resources.

Financial markets in a capitalist society need to experience regular minor stresses to develop the capacity to withstand larger problems. Therefore you cannot strictly control the flow of capital which needs to be as free as possible.

Over periods of prolonged prosperity, capitalist economies tend to move from a financial structure dominated by hedge finance to a structure that increasingly emphasises speculative finance. Debts exceed what borrowers can pay off from their incoming revenues, which in turns produces a financial crisis.

While the all-powerful profit motive dominates the global economy, there is a new and very far-reaching economy that's sprung up in the last decades that is trying something different. It is the cooperative economy.

While each cooperative is run differently, they all have the same characteristic: democracy in the workplace. There is no all, powerful CEO determining the pay for himself and his workers, there is no secret board of directors looking out for the best interest of unknown shareholders.

A cooperative is managed and owned by its workers. Usually through a small fee, an employee can buy a stake in the co-op and be part of the decision-making process-one person, one vote. As business gets better, the profits don't go to the very top, they are spread among the workers, providing incentives for everyone to work harder and sell more together-hence the name "cooperative".

To eradicate poverty and to reduce economic inequality we must move away from the capitalist, competitive, "growth first" model of development and toward a new model that places survival of humans and the environment before the needs of corporate profit and technological advancement. We need sustainable and democratic models of development that honour social, ethical and ecological principles, including the essential oneness and equality of all human beings.

We need people to wake up and realise the earth is not infinite and the economists should put a realistic price on limited resources such as land, oil and water. We must regulate abuses within capitalism. How do we stop pollution? How do we stop waste? Clues to these and other important questions are found throughout this book.

Demographics

Demographics tell us a typical household

spends the most money when the head of the household is forty-six-when, on average, the parents see their kids leaving the nest. To understand the broad economic trends we have to recognise the fact that new generations of consumers enter the workforce around age twenty and spend more money as they raise their families, buy houses and cars, borrow, and so on.

The average family borrows the most when the parents are age forty-one, they spend the most at age forty-six, save the most at age fifty-four and have the highest net worth at age sixty-four. After the age of fifty five spending drops like a rock all the way into death.

Demographics shows consumer spending patterns over the course of their life cycle. Consumers may peak at a different age but the trend is undeniable. It's about the predictable things people do as they age.

9. Globalisation

Globalisation is the processes of international integrating of world views, products, ideas, trade and transactions, capital and investment movements, migration and the dissemination of knowledge.

Things You Should Know

Mercantilism was the dominant economic model of the seventeenth through nineteenth centuries. Mercantilism is the opposite of globalisation. It adherently relies on closed markets and closed capital accounts to achieve their goal of accumulating wealth at the expense of others.

Classical mercantilism main principle was that wealth was tangible and found in land, commodities and gold. The acquisition of wealth is a zero-sum game in which wealth acquired by one nation comes at the expense of others.

Trading is done with friendly partners to the exclusion of rivals. Subsidies and discrimination are legitimate tools to achieve economic goals. Success in mercantilism was measured by the accumulation of gold.

The period between 1870 and 1914 was the first globalization with almost no inflation due to technology innovations, increased productivity, and rising living standards without increasing unemployment.

Globalisation led to more innovation as there is an incentive to invest more in research and development because the rewards of finding the right product to sell to a global population are that much greater. The second globalization began in 1989 with the end of the Cold War.

Free trade is achieved by a group of countries that have signed an agreement, which eliminates tariffs, import quotas, and preference on most goods and services traded between them. If people are also free to move between the countries, in addition to a free-trade area, it would be considered an open border.

The rich countries try to convince everyone that wealth is the product of competition. The shocking truth is that every economically successful society has been guilty in its formative stages of protectionism. Britain taxed exports of raw wool and imports of clothing in the sixteenth century in order to nurture its export-orientated woollen textiles industry. France introduced similar strategies in the seventeenth century. America used high tariffs on imports from the early days until the early twentieth century to protect its industries.

These countries focused a lot of state support on a small group of large firms- monopolies and oligopolies- which had the ability to obtain large capital investments and compete internationally.

Protectionism is expensive and inefficient because it adds cost, punishes consumers and invites retaliation. However, as a means to the long-term end of industrial learning, protectionism makes possible the acquisition of strategically vital knowledge at a cost that is only temporary

Between the period of 1600 and 1800 trade was increased when the maritime European empires were established. The companies were often described as the first multinational corporations in which stock was offered. The sudden abundance of cheap energy (oil) further enhanced the growth of industrialisation, speculation urbanisation and globalisation as the rapid population growth created sustained demand for commodities.

In 1944, 44 nations attended the Bretton Woods Conference with a purpose of stabilising world currencies and establishing credit for international trade in the post World War II era. The conference established many of the organisations essential goals to advance towards a close-knit global economy and global financial system, such as the World Bank, the International Monetary Fund, and the International Trade Organisation.

Current globalisation trends can be largely accounted for by developed economies integrating with less developed economies as the world society offers a complex web of forces and factors that bring people, cultures, markets, beliefs and practices into increasingly greater proximity to one another.

The current globalisation emerged not through the initiation of any new policies but through the elimination of many old ones. From the end of World War II to the end of the Cold

War, the world had been divided not only by the Iron Curtain separating the communist and capitalist spheres but also by restrictions imposed by capitalist countries themselves. The world was highly fragmented, discriminatory and costly for firms with international ambitions.

Non–trading developing states such as the former Soviet Union, China before 1978 and India before 1991 made painfully slow technological progress: indeed so much so that their population lost faith in the possibilities of economic advancement.

Deregulation caused a massive overhaul of the world's trading rules and the international commerce took off. Initially, export-orientated Asian nations were the biggest winners in the post-Cold War embrace of global capitalism. Their rapid expanding economies gathered foreign investment.

While the dollar and other major currencies of the world continued to freely float against each other, the Asian monetary authorities committed themselves to fixed exchange rate regimes.

They intervened in the market if their currencies moved outside a preordained range against the dollar. Their seemingly stable exchange rates gave local banks a sense of stability which gained them easy and cheap access to foreign loans.

During the period between 1991 and 2009 three hundred million people have escaped extreme poverty and joined the middle class as globalisation increased wealth for poor countries. A strong middle class with well-paying jobs and high purchasing power ensures economic stability.

Never before in human history have so many people been lifted out of absolute poverty. Nor have there been so many entrants into global middle class. Simple things like a flush toilet, electricity at home, a cell phone, a TV set, and a refrigerator have represented the aspirations of billions. For a long time, they seemed out of reach. Now many, if not most people believe that these aspirations are achievable.

For centuries, less than 1% of the world's population enjoyed sufficient income to spend it on anything beyond basic needs. The United Nations calculated that the average income world-wide have risen by 70% since 1980, reaching just over $10,000 per person in 2011. The growth has been spectacular in developing countries even more so in India and China. The two gigantic nations representing over a third of the globe's population has given unprecedented improvement in living standards of their people in a space of a generation.

Economists called this the "New Economy" allowing for faster and longer non-inflationary growth periods of low unemployment.

The internet and communication revolution led to quantum leaps in the efficiency with which goods were produced around the world.

Technology gave more people the opportunity to acquire knowledge and improve themselves. In the space of just more than a decade the mobile phone has gone a long way to close the telecommunication gap between the rich and poor parts of the planet.

China's broadband subscribers grew from 10 million in 2000 to 120 million in 2010 and its mobile phone usage surged from 100 million to 824 million making China by far the biggest user of both services.

Even in the slums of Rio de Janeiro almost everyone has a mobile phone. In India it has gone from virtually zero to 72% (752million) from 1999 to 2011. Latin America has seen the biggest rise: in Brazil the proportion has hit 123% of the population, due to the number of people with more than one mobile.

Adding up the total number of all phones, mobile and fixed-line, phone ownership in the rich countries rose from 93% of the population in 1999 to 155% in 2010. The mobile phone has been a great convenience; it has improved productivity, how we undertake research and how we engage with other people.

The emerging markets had a more profound experience with globalisation. Brazil, Russia, India, China and South Africa (BRICS) came into their own in the first decade of the new millennium as they embraced free market policies and tapped into the opportunities of an ever-broadening global market place.

While advanced countries concentrated on finance and services the emerging economies created new manufacturing industries while rapidly improving the quality and sophistication of their output. This enabled them to add value and increase earning power.

As for the developed world, the economic performance was respectable and the population grew richer. This caused the longest and most stable boom since the 1960's and the era was labelled by the economists as the "Great Moderation"

Inflation in the U.S., EU and UK fell from double-digit rates of the 1970s and 1980s and stayed down due to the following;

a) Imports of far cheaper goods from China and similar low-cost manufacturing economies in Asia.

b) Interest rates kept at record low levels by

central banks.

c) Consumers in developed countries borrowing too much to finance their excessive consumption.

International tourist arrivals have shown virtually uninterrupted growth: from 25 million in 1950, to 277 million in 1980, to 435 million in 1990, to 675 million in 2000, and the current 940 million. It is estimated that international arrivals will reach 1.6 billion by 2020. In short, one in five inhabitants of planet earth will travel across an international boundary.

Although globalisation is about greater flows of goods and services it does not necessarily apply to emigration. The number of legal migrants has increased from 2.3% in 1965 to 3.1% in 2010 as most countries still maintain strict immigration controls.

Illegal migration across the world on an unprecedented scale is underway. Mexico is exploding into America; and North Africa overflowing into Europe while China seems destined to unload some of her population into the wide empty spaces.

The world's wealthiest cities attract the biggest cross-border influxes and in some cases the foreign-born population forms the majority of the population.

When the World Trade Organisation agreed

to open up the textile markets in Europe, Chinese exporters jumped the gun and increased their exports to 5 times in pullovers and 4.5 times in trousers that year to Europe. When the European textile distributors cried out and insist on quotas to protect their industries, the Chinese exporters replied with the following, 'quotas won't keep consumers warm this winter'.

Notwithstanding job losses in the European textile industry, the public supported free trade. The public are not concerned about job losses or the working conditions of the Chinese workers, as their focus is on low priced items from China.

Western dependency on cheap products will grow. Nations of the world have been subjected to a set of values and short term thinking within which they are embedded, and are dangerously close to collapse.

Europe's problems with Chinese imports have a centuries-long history. Already in the seventeen hundreds the Jesuits reckoned that in the Shanghai area alone there were 200,000 weavers of calicoes, by far higher than was in Europe. Before long exports to Europe grew until a million pieces were shipped to Britain and America by the beginning of the nineteenth century.

Due to the globalisation of trade and

business ventures, the trends of various stock markets around the world no longer move in isolation. The market downturn in one large economy may send other stock markets into bear market territory even if their economies are not directly affected

Trade is no longer just about moving physical objects around the globe. With the help of modern telecommunications, trade in services-finance, law, software, telesales, tourism, construction expertise-has really taken off. Worldwide trade in services quadrupled between 1980 and 2010, and accounts for about 20% of total trade these days.

From 1977 to 2008 the world's nominal GDP grew by 7 times. The value of foreign exchange trading has increased from eleven times the value of global trade in 1980 to seventy-tree times in 2010. Mind-boggling quantities of currencies are being traded for reasons that have almost nothing to do with the needs of most businesses and households.

Globalisation diminished the regulatory clout which governments wield over the increasingly borderless banks. Financial institutions can move billions of dollars across borders in seconds. Slowly world leaders are beginning to acknowledge that some global rules may actually benefit and enhance the world interests.

The annual foreign currency exchange is about one quadrillion which is sixteen times the value of everything produced in the world during the same period, far more than needed to pay for all the world's trade. This is because of the high-stakes betting on markets, the financial speculation of banks and financial institutions.

It is increasingly clear that capital markets and trade liberalisation programs made it far easier for wealthy people and corporations to evade taxes and help hide the transfer of money illicitly into bank accounts and offshore trusts. This behaviour of self-indulgence and short-term thinking are made without foresight and without due care.

The large corporations and banks requires exponentially increasing amounts of money, so much that in the end it will consume everything in sight until it devours themselves.

What is the impact on planet earth? Globalisation could be short-term thinking as long-term concerns about where society is heading or the possible costs involved are set aside.

Rapid industrialisation has resulted in equally rapid environment decay. Deserts are encroaching on agricultural land, ancient forests are being destroyed, soil fertility is in decline, water shortages are reaching a crisis point and cities are choking on smog and pollution.

A study recently released by the Blacksmith Institute reveals, for the first time ever, the impact of industrial pollutants on communities across the planet. It found that industrial-waste dump sites containing toxic horrors such as lead, mercury, and chromium poison more than 125 million people in forty-nine different low- and middle-income nations around the planet. The report says, industrial pollution is now a bigger global health problem for the world than malaria and tuberculosis.

Those against globalisation said it was a method of Western business leaders and investors to exploit the rest of the world's cheap labour and natural resources for their own selfish enrichment. This leads to the next topic of global environment versus the global consumer.

There is a growing global consensus that humanity is now seriously threatening the fragile environment of our planet. The global environment is being threatened in many dimensions; rainforests, fishery stocks, water supply, over population, air pollution and many more.

Other things being equal, a larger population will eat more food, drink more water, wear more clothes, occupy more shelter, and generate more excrement than a smaller one. That's an indisputable biological fact.

Infinite growth is impossible on a finite planet. We are aware of the environment vulnerability and a fast expanding middle class on the globe. We cannot have both. We can either take care of our planet, or we can rapidly expand our global middle class, but which? It is ethical to save our planet but it is equally ethical to elevate people from poverty.

"We know that the world is burning. The question is how to put out the fire." Twilly Cannon, former captain of the Greenpeace ship, Rainbow Warrior.

The environment crisis demands rapid and decisive action, but we can't act effectively unless we clearly understand what is causing the crisis. If we misdiagnose the illness, at best we will waste precious time on ineffective cures; at worst we will do even more damage.

Just as we though it cannot get worse, think again. With a few exceptions the family dynasty has ruled over the people during the human history.

For the rich and powerful, the family unit has been the principal institution through which power is accumulated preserved and propagated because the interest is multigenerational, regarding long-term planning and strategy. In powerful states and empires, families have been essential in the process of constructing and governing the major institutions within those societies and in direct control of the state structure.

This has been the case for most of our history and yet in the modern era, we imagine our societies to be free of dynastic rule- something long past not consistent with the ideals and functions of democracy capitalism. We might imagine this to be true, but we would be in fact be wrong.

Dynastic power not only remains, but it evolves and adapts. In the present world of 'globalisation' with the money-central banking system the world is largely dominated by a single state, the USA acting on behalf of the dynastic families who controls the powerful corporations and financial institutions. Their power is not in direct control of the political apparatus but in their concentration of control over the financial, economic and industrial spheres.

They keep the politics of dynastic power from being understood or contemplated by the masses. We are distracted with sports, entertainment, royal weddings, a fear of foreigners and terrorism, and are blinded and manipulated by a deeply embedded propaganda system.

Corporate America is seen as the self-made rich of the supposedly democratic capitalist society. The reality is that a third of the world's largest multinational corporations are in fact family businesses mostly run by family members. Dynastic trusts allow super-rich families to provide their heirs with money and property largely free from taxes and immune to the claims of creditors.

Early in 2012, the Rothschild family, with various banks and investment entities spread out across multiple European nations and family branches, was making a concerted effort to begin the process of 'merging its French and British assets into a single entity, aiming to secure 'long-term control over the family's 'international banking empire'.

10. Why Are Some Countries Poor?

Scholars have been debating for centuries why some countries stay consistently poor while others prosper. Wars as a reason are obviously excluded. Some had a hypothesis which claims that the great divide between the rich and poor countries is created by geographical differences. Many poor countries, such as those in Africa, Central America and South Asia, are between the tropics of Cancer and Capricorn. Rich nations, in contrast, tend to be in temperate latitudes.

The French political philosopher Montesquieu argued that people in tropical climates tended to be lazy and lack inquisitiveness. As a consequence, they didn't work hard and were not innovative, and this was the reason they were poor. He also speculated that lazy people tended to be ruled by despots, suggesting that a tropical location could explain not just poverty but also some of the political phenomena associated with economic failure, such as dictatorship.

History illustrates that there is no simple or enduring connection between climate or geography and economic success. At the time of the conquest of the Americas by Columbus, the great Aztec and Inca civilizations were politically centralised and complex. The Aztecs traded with money and were able to read and write. Both civilizations had built roads and provided famine relief while people living in the current America and Canada were mostly inhabited by Stone Age civilizations.

The theory that hot countries are intrinsically poor, though contradicted by recent rapid economic advance of countries such as Singapore and Malaysia is still forcefully advocated by some, such as the economist Jeffrey Sachs. The modern version of this view emphasizes not the direct effects of climate on work effort or thought processes, but two additional arguments: first, those tropical diseases, particularly malaria, have very adverse consequences for health and therefore labour productivity; and second, that tropical soils do not allow for productive agriculture. The conclusion, though, is the same: temperate climates have a relative advantage over tropical and semitropical areas.

World inequality cannot be explained by climate or diseases, or any version of the geography hypothesis as it cannot explain differences between the north and south of Nogales, or North and South Korea, or those between East and West Germany before the fall of the Berlin Wall, South and North America.

Jared Diamond, an ecologist and evolutionary biologist argued that the inequality rested in different historical endowments of plant and animal species which influenced agricultural productivity. In some areas were a large number of species that could be domesticated by humans. Having many species capable of being domesticated made it very logical for societies to make the transition from hunter-gatherer to a farming lifestyle. Therefore, where farming dominated, technological innovation took place much more rapidly than in other parts of the world.

Though Diamond's thesis is a powerful approach to the puzzle on which he focuses, it cannot be extended to explain modern world inequality. He argued that the Spanish were able to dominate the civilizations of the Americas because of their longer history of farming and consequent superior technology. It does not explain why the Mexicans and Peruvians inhabiting the former lands of the Aztecs and Incas are poor.

The German sociologist, Max Weber wrote that ethic played a key role in facilitating the rise of modern industrial society in Western Europe. The culture hypothesis relies on beliefs, values and ethics as well. They believe that Africans are poor because they lack a good work ethic. Other aspects, such as the extent to which people trust each other or are able to cooperate, are also important in determining wealth.

In the list of the thirty poorest counties in the world today, you will find almost all of them in sub-Saharan Africa. Historically, sub-Saharan Africa was poorer than most other parts of the world, and their ancestors did not develop the wheel, writing, or the plough. They were very quick to accept one venerable Western innovation: the gun. It might be true today that Africans trust each other less than people in other parts of the world. This is the outcome of a long history of lacking proper institutions which have undermined human and property rights in Africa.

Nations fail today due to economic failure

which prevents people to save, invest, and be innovative. Not only fail their leaders to provide security and public services but they are just too happy to extract resources or suppress any type of independent economic activity that threatens themselves and the economic elites.

In some extreme cases, such as Zimbabwe, Sri Lanka and Sierra Leone the leaders pave the way for complete state failure, destroying not only law and order but also even the most basic economic incentives. The result is economic stagnation leading to violence against civilians, civil wars, mass displacements, famines and epidemics, making those countries even poorer.

It might be hard to understand how a situation like this can sustain itself for decades. This symbiotic relationship arises because national politicians exploit the lawlessness in peripheral parts of the country, while paramilitary groups are left to their own devices by the national government.

A popular theory held by most economists is that world inequality exists because it is almost impossible to eradicate poverty. They follow Lionel Robbins, an English economist who proposed that "economics as a science which studies human behaviour as a relationship between ends and scarce means which have alternative uses."

André Klopper

The science of economics should focus on the best use of scarce means to satisfy social ends. The First Welfare Theorem identifies the circumstances under which the allocation of resources in a "market economy" is socially desirable from an economic point of view.

In a free market all individuals and firms can freely produce, buy and sell any products and services that they wish. When these circumstances are not present there is a "market failure." Such failures provide the basis for a theory of world inequality; since the more that market failures go un-addressed the poorer a country is likely to be.

Therefore, countries are poor because they have a lot of market failures and their leaders do not rectify the problems. Another problem is due to the consequence of the ownership structure of the land and the incentives that are created for farmers by the governments and institutions under which they live.

Inequality in the modern world largely results from uneven dissemination and adoption of technologies caused by "market failure". Those in un-checked power of poor countries build structures to ensure the continuity of their power which creates poverty for the masses.

The policies are to enrich a few at the

expense of many. Those who benefits have the resources to build their own private armies, to buy their judges, and to rig their elections to remain in power,

The prolonged conflict between the rich elite and the depressed masses turns into bloody civil wars which create further economic ruin and human suffering.

Throughout the last five decades, hundreds of billions of dollars have been paid to governments around the world as "development" aid. The citizens of many Western nations feel guilt and unease about the economic and humanitarian disasters around the world, and foreign aid makes them believe that something is being done to combat the problems.

Out of every dollar given to aid, less than 10 cents makes it to the poorest people in the world. Much of it has been wasted in overheads and corruption. It is ineffective as it will be stolen and very unlikely be delivered where it's supposed to go. In the worst-case scenario, it will be pocketed by the very people that are causing the root of the problems of these societies.

Foreign aid is not a very effective means of dealing with the failure of nations around the world today. The countries need different political institutions to break out of the cycle of poverty.

In 1750, the average living standard all around the world was about the same. Now the standards between the developed countries and the developing countries aren't even close. The wealth of the developed countries is based, in large measure, on centuries of systematic plunder of the developing countries, a process that continues to this day. Part of that process has been the transfer of polluting industries to the developing countries, where they aren't subject to environmental protection regulations.

In Nigeria, oil drilling has caused immense damage to the Niger Delta, home to about thirty million people. Each year more oil is spilled into the delta than was spilled in the Gulf of Mexico oil disaster of 2010.

In Ecuador thirty thousand indigenous people are suing oil giant Chevron for $113 billion to clean up the shocking damage done to the Amazon rainforest. The devastation has been called a "Rainforest Chernobyl." Over three decades, Chevron has dumped billions litters of contaminated water into the area's rivers and left behind about a thousand open pits of toxic waste.

The rainforest ecosystem has been irreparably damaged and the groundwater polluted. Cancer, birth defects, and miscarriages have reached epidemic proportions in nearby indigenous communities.

11. The Federal Reserve

The U.S. Federal Reserve System is the most powerful central bank in history and the dominant force in the U.S. economy today. However, the Federal Reserve is not actually federal, and it keeps no reserves.

The Federal Reserve is commonly called the 'Fed' confusing it with the U.S. government; but it is actually a private corporation consisting of twelve regional Federal Reserve banks. It is so private that its stock is not even traded on the stock exchange. It is owned by a consortium of private banks, the biggest of which are Citibank and J.P. Morgan Chase Company. The Rothschild family owns 52% of the Federal Reserve.

J.P. Morgan and William Rockefeller come together with a few other influential people in a secret rendezvous to devise a banking scheme that would benefit them. They knew if it leaked out that they had written a banking bill, it would never be passed by congress.

When the Aldrich Bill was brought before the congress it was defeated by the congressional opposition that was strongly against any bill suggesting a central bank or control by Wall Street money. Morgan had another problem besides the opposition in Congress, President Taft who took vengeance on Morgan by filing antitrust suits to break up the two leading Morgan trusts.

Taft was sure to be re-elected but Morgan deliberately created a new party, the Progressive Party and brought Theodore Roosevelt out of retirement to run as its candidate. Roosevelt took enough votes away from Taft to allow Morgan to get his real candidate W. Wilson elected as president. Roosevelt knew he was duped and the Progressive Party was liquidated.

False rumours were spread causing a major bank panic and the Aldrich Bill was changed to the Federal Reserve Act which was brought to Congress three days before Christmas, when the members were preoccupied with departure for the holidays and in their haste agreed that the country needed a central banking system to stop future panics.

The bill passed on December 22, 1913, President Wilson signed it into law the next day. Later he regretted what he had done. He is reported to have said before he died, "I have unwittingly ruined my country."

The creation of the Federal Reserve System

was a major coup for it granted the very rich of the world (J.P Morgan and John D. Rockefeller and the Rothschilds) the power to control the money supply of the United States.

The Fed is a banking cartel run by some of the most powerful men in the financial world. The creation of the Fed was basically a license to print money.

Another reason the Federal Reserve System was created was to protect the biggest banks from failing by providing liquidity to those banks when they are in financial trouble, which protected the wealth of the rich, not of the taxpayers.

In very simple terms the Fed can only do two things. They are:

1. Create money out of thin air.

2. Lend money they do not have. When you borrow money from the bank, the bank does not need to have that money in the vault.

The commission which examined the 2008 financial crisis reached the conclusion that regulatory failure was a primary cause of the crisis and it laid that failure squarely at the feet of the Fed. All of the Fed's failures were avoidable.

As the Fed pile on more leverage on their capital base they are well aware that if their assets decline in value by 2%, a fairly small event in volatile markets, it will wipe out their capital, and they would be insolvent.

Ironically, the world is looking to the Federal Reserve and the U.S. Treasury to solve our money problems, even though those institutions are causing the problems.

The Fed has failed to maintain price stability, failed as lender of last resort, failed to maintain full employment, failed as a bank regulator and failed to preserve the integrity of its balance sheet. It also failed to prevent the debasement of the U.S. dollar.

The modern reserve/central banks have three notable flaws;

1. It depends on perception. Just like the entire banking system they are also worth only a fraction of the claims against it.

2. It inevitably destroys its currency. Today's system can create virtually unlimited amounts of credit. But credit is not wealth.

3. It distorts markets and misallocates resources. As they dispensed with sound money altogether, leaving only the bank-created paper in circulation which resulted in a system based on force rather than choice, in attempt to maintain the illusion of fiat currency safety and

soundness.

12. World Bankers

Most of the people around the globe are aware that the Vatican in Rome does not fall under the jurisdiction of Rome nor Italy. However, very few people know that the London financial district in London and Washington D.C. in the United States are not part of the countries where they exist, but are independent "city states" with their own laws and constitution and fly their own flags.

The tiny area of a little over one square mile in the heart of London is called the city of London while London city is the metropolis. The city of London is headed by the Lord Mayor of the city of London, an office separate from the Mayor of London who heads the London metropolitan city.

The city of London is not subject to regulation by the British Parliament and is in effect a sovereign world power which is controlled by the Rothschild family who considers them as legal owner of this planet.

Within the city of London are the Bank of England, the Stock Exchange and many institutions of world-wide scope. The City carries on its business of local government with fanciful display of pompous medieval ceremony and with its officers, attire in grotesque ancient costumes. Its voting power is vested in secret guilds.

The City, through its ruling power of the "Crown" and it's all powerful Bank of England, holds the purse-strings of the British Empire; the Parliament still holds the taxing power within the British Isles, and the disposition, of the citizens of Great Britain.

The Bank of England was set up under the control of Nathan Rothschild in the financial district known as the city of London. The Bank of England is not subject to any control by any governmental agency of Great Britain, and it is above the government, despite the fact that it is privately owned and its directors are nominated by its proprietors.

. "The City" operates as a super-government of the world; and no incident occurs in any part of the world without its participation in some form. "The City' is bolstered by huge funds being syphoned out of the treasury of the United States.

The American Wall Street in New York became a branch office of the Bank of England in 1896. The National Banking Act of 1863 delivered a monopoly over the power to create the nation's money supply to the Wall Street bankers and their European affiliates. The powerful British bankers funded the Confederates in the Civil War through the Wall Street Bank.

"Let me issue and control a nation's money," Amschel Rothschild boasted in 1790, "and I care not who writes its laws."

Who was this Amschel Rothschild? The House of Rothschild was founded in Frankfurt in the mid-eighteenth century, when a moneylender named Mayer Amschel Bauer changed his name to Amschel Rothschild and fathered ten children. His five sons were sent to the major capitals of Europe to open branches for the family banking business. They opened banks in London, Paris, Vienna, Berlin and Naples.

The family fortunes got a major boost in 1815, when Nathan in London led the British investors to believe that Britain had lost against Napoleon at the Battle of Waterloo. Within hours the British government bond prices plummeted and Nathan bough the entire stock of government bonds.

Over the course of the nineteenth century, N.M. Rothschild would become the biggest bank of the world, and the five brothers would come to control most of the foreign-loan business of Europe.

The Rothschilds financed the Rockefeller and Morgan rivals in America who competed for power in the political scene. In 1850 Junius Morgan became a partner in a London investment business specialising in transactions between Britain and the United States. His son John became head of the firm's New York branch which was named J.P Morgan & Co. His son became a partner in the branch in London.

Roosevelt understood that since the American Revolution the world has been ruled by the very wealthy as he called them the "Economic Royalists". Today, these people are often referred to as "the 1 percent", but they are only a tiny fraction of the top 1 percent.

Their greed made the War of Independence inevitable. They pulled the strings of both the North and South during the Civil War. They provoked the stock market crash of 1929 triggering the Great depression. In fact, the world history is one of constant struggle against this cultural infection.

The rich elite used monopolies in steel, oil, rail and finance to dominate the American economy. They built massive monopolies while ruthlessly destroying any upstart that dared to compete. There was big money to be made in post-Civil War America. The nation's GDP nearly doubled, growing fast but the wealth didn't trickle down as the rich have mastered monopoly while the rest of America was going bankrupt.

In powerful states and empires, families have been essential in the process of constructing and governing the major institutions within those societies as well as in the direct control of the imperial or state structure itself. Whether headed by emperors, kings, queens or sultans, family dynasties have very often exerted direct political control over society.

This has been the case for much of human history, at least as long as empires and states have been consistent features. Yet today we imagine our societies to be free of dynastic rule as it is no longer consistent with the ideals and functions of democracy, capitalism or modernity. We might imagine this to be true, but we would in fact be wrong.

As political and economic spheres opened up, new structures emerged to centralise power within those spheres. As the rulers handed over the ultimate authority to issue coins to other institutions, merchants and financiers stepped in to increase their influence over the new institutions and a changing world order.

Their power was not directly in control of the political apparatus but their concentration of control was over the financial, economic and industrial spheres. With that power inevitably come both the desire and the ability to influence and pressure the political sphere.

Today it is the industrial, financial and corporate dynasties that have risen to unparalleled positions of authority in the age of globalisation.

The super-elite do not make their fortunes public therefore they are not on the Forbes Magazine richest list. The Rothschilds, the Rockefellers, the Warburgs, and a long list of royal families consider it to be either in bad taste or because they fear retribution from the bottom of the wealth pyramid.

The small number of individuals controls the political campaign contributions, and has progressively corrupted the U.S. government and political system. The political corruption has in turn further entrenched the wealthy and financial sector that became a major driver of economic and social decline.

The wealthy are safeguarded from instability, and declining services while the bottom sixty-six per cent of the population has become less educated, less informed, less prosperous, angrier, and even more cynical about its political leadership.

While the super-rich are amassing fortunes rivalling the economics of small countries, the total wealth of the average American family is $57,000. Convert that into hundred dollar bills, and it's a stack about two inches tall. People earning an income of $300,000 a year earn a stack every year that is about a foot high. The average wealth of billionaires on the Forbes 400 list is $4.2 billion. Convert that into a stack of hundred-dollar bills and it would reach over two miles in the sky. Although that is incredible the combined wealth of the top five families measured in a stack of hundred dollar bills would reach several thousand miles in the sky.

In a January 2012 article called "Who Rules America?" Professor James Petras wrote, "Today it is said 2% of the households own 80% of the world's assets." These private equity banks are involved in every sector of the economy, in every region of the world economy and increasingly speculate in the conglomerates which are required. Much of the investment funds now in the hands of U.S. investment banks, hedge funds and other sectors of the financial ruling class originated in profits extracted from workers in the manufacturing and service sector.

One third of the Fortune 500 companies are in fact family businesses. Dynastic trusts allow super-rich families to provide their heirs with money and property largely free from taxes for generations in perpetuity.

One of the world's most famous family

trusts-is that of Rockefeller & Co., now known as Rockefeller Financial. It was founded in 1882 by the oil baron-industrialist John D. Rockefeller as the "family office" to manage the Rockefeller family investments and wealth. By 2008 the trust had roughly US$28 billion under management for multiple clients.

Early in 2012, the Rothschild family, with various banks and investment entities spread out across multiple European nations and family branches and began to merge its French and British assets into a single entity to secure long term control over the family's international banking empire. The main goal of the merger was provide the family a 57 per cent share in the voting rights to protect the merged entity from hostile takeovers.

Thus when Lord (Jacob) Rothschild-who manages the British Rothschild family trust, RIT Capital Partners-announced that RIT would be purchasing a 37 per cent stake in Rockefeller Financial Services in May 2012 for an "undisclosed sum" it was announced as a "strategic partnership" that would allow the Rothschilds to unite the two family patriarchs of David Rockefeller and Jacob Rothschild "whose personal relationship spans five decades."

The world's super-rich families compete and cooperate for control not just over nations but over entire regions and the planet as a whole. Globalisation has facilitated the widespread reach of the "family office" now the central institution of modern family dynasties.

13. The Rise And Fall Of The United States

The Great Depression caused a very high unemployment rate which led to a drastic drop in labour rates. This caused the labour force in a subordinate position enabling the manufactures a period of rapid expansion and high profits. The huge profits ensured large surpluses which provided enough investment for the further growth of productivity and real wages.

Under the stimulus of a powerful wartime demand, the U.S economy was able to secure unprecedentedly high profit rates that made a powerful expansion, and increased its already impressive lead over all other national economies.

America's economy took off during the time when Japan and Western Europe were torn apart by war. As the war had devastated most of the U.S.'s competitors it faced no serious competition for a quater of a century after the war.

This rapid growth of the U.S. caused the nation to become so wealthy and powerful that it achieved global dominance without seeming even to try. Productivity rose and working people's wages rose. Average Americans were getting richer while a third of the workforce was unionised. Working-class people bought homes and cars, had affordable health care, and took vacations. By the 1960s, a solid middle class had emerged.

The average and largely unsophisticated factory-workers and particularly their teenage children had more time and money on their hands. Idle hands with free college led to civil and social rights movements.

As a consequence of the very developments with which America obtained its leading position, their economy found it difficult to sustain its high levels of investment growth. They became complacent, rigid, highly inefficient oligopolies or even in some cases monopolies.

The American economy eased from the end of the Korean War, by a loss of momentum, manifested in a slowdown of capital accumulation.

The rising of local labour costs and the profit-making opportunities during the boom in Western Europe caused U.S. companies to invest abroad. The other countries provided substantial levels of protection for home industries with undervalued currencies while imposing limits on the international mobility of capital.

This led to huge gains in productive effectiveness in the other countries which was a sharp contrast to the relatively slow-growing U.S economy. The U.S companies penetrated the overseas market more by relocating their industries through multinational corporations and banks rather than export goods and services. The U.S government supported this liberalisation of the world economy at the expense of their domestic based manufacturing.

Within two decades after World War II German and Japanese manufactures were able to achieve the extraordinary rates of export growth that drove their economies forward by gaining a greater share in the world export market and even penetrate the enormous U.S market itself. They were able to do this with relatively advanced techniques and low wages to reduce costs to maintain high profits while the U.S. manufacturers had over-invested and were caught with inflexible costs, fixed production methods and high wages. This led to the relative decline of the U.S. domestic economy.

The U.S. government was willing to tolerate their rivals' high level of state interventions, their trade protections, their undervalued exchange rates as they had an interest in their rivals' economic development and their political stability. The declining manufacturing competitiveness of the U.S. led to a deficit in their trading balance while the trading balance in Japan and Germany grew.

The trade deficit was expanding monthly as American consumers gravitated towards cheap new imports from Europe and Japan. A growing band of nervous foreign investors began exchanging their dollar reserves for gold, driving U.S. gold holdings down to dangerously low levels.

President Nixon felt trapped by an economic juggernaut he could not control. He gave a televised address to the American people about the war by international money speculators. He dropped the gold standard, the fixed exchange rates were discarded and the U.S. dollar was sharply devalued. The immediate impact was a collapse in world stock prices. The oil embargo produced an exponential increase in energy prices.

During the long term downturn between the 1970's and the mid-1990s, the growth of investment fell sharply; unemployment increased, and reduced productivity all during the time of a succession of recessions and financial crises.

After a confused failed reformed attempt by

President Jimmy Carter, American politics turned increasingly towards deriving their power by appealing to popular prejudices and corruption. The politicians pretended that the problem was taxes and excessive government, while using deficit spending and financial bubbles to cover up America's long term problems.

Both political parties tilted ever more towards the financial sector, the very wealthy and the most powerful, most concentrated industry in the U.S.

By the late 1980's Japan had definitively surpassed the U.S. not only in the car industry but also in machine tools and robotics, as well as in their advanced use in a variety of manufacturing sectors. Similarly, Japanese excellence in producing commodity semiconductors and liquid crystal displays pulled along its semiconductor capital equipment industry.

The Japanese industry also engaged in large-scale technology licensing, copying, and intellectual property theft, aided by Japanese industrial policy which protected the domestic markets from uncontrolled foreign competition.

During a PBS television special: Even though Americans comprise only five percent of the world's population, in 1996 they used nearly a third of its resources and produced almost half of its hazardous waste. The average North American consumes five times as much as an average Mexican, 10 times as much as an average Chinese and 30 times as much as the average person in India.

By the year 2000 the U.S. was still universally considered as the super power in the world, and with the most advanced technology base, most dominant military, and dominated the Internet industry. With the former Soviet Union in collapse and China converted to government-led capitalism, America's growth continued. America could do no wrong.

However, the fall of the mighty is a classic theme of tragedy. Many countries had obtained dominance in their area just to lose it again. However, when America's dominance was waning people asked themselves, how could this happen?

The majority of people blame the Bush administration who squandered the Americans wealth on wars and tax cuts for the wealthy while letting the banks run wild. Then the Bush administration left the mess to Obama, who is getting the economy into a worse condition while struggling to pick up the pieces.

Bush with his dishonesty, greed, and stupidity devastated America's finances with his fraudulently orchestrated incompetently managed wars and enormous tax cuts.

However, to put all the blame on him and Obama would be wrong.

The whole truth is that for the last forty years America has slowly eroded its power and prestige. There have been occasional episodes of real progress such as the Internet revolution; computer science and entrepreneurial skills which lifted America, but the dominant trend has been in decline.

Living standards of the American people have been damaged by wars in Korea, Vietnam, Iraq and Afghanistan. Today, as people all over the world read what is happening over the globe most of them concur that the American lead wars have become intolerable.

Competition is destroyed by unrestrained growth of corporate interests. Big companies buy small companies until there are no small businesses left. Private-equity firms take care of the rest, even harvesting small- and medium-sized businesses for a profit.

There is absolutely no reason to believe that bigger companies are more efficient, but that is what happened in America. This happened in the financial services, the energy sector, telecommunication sector, retailing, information technology, automotive industry, and media and entertainment industries. They are all dominated by four or less huge corporations in each industry.

Large firms in concentrated industries have much more bargaining power relative to employees and suppliers. They became known for being brutally tough on their suppliers, forcing them to cut costs, and their low wage workforce. The huge incomes of management in giant corporations compared to the low salaries of the workforce caused a bigger income inequality.

The structural concentration of American industries has continued over the last forty years during which the economic power in the U.S. also became more concentrated at the individual level, with a small minority of households owning the majority of financial wealth.

The economic and social insecurity produced anger, desperation and strikes from the workforce. There are places all across America that have already crashed leaving ghost towns because all the work was outsourced to low-wage nations. There's nothing left. There is no employment. Whole blocks are abandoned. The only thing functioning are open–air drug markets.

Between 2000 and 2009, multinationals cut 2.9 million jobs in the United States and added 2.4 million jobs overseas. Although it doesn't prove a casually connection, it would be surprising if those were two completely unrelated numbers. From 1991 to 2007, U.S imports from China rose from $26 billion to about $330 billion. To some extent the losses in the job market are made up by lower prices for outsourced goods for the U.S. consumers but it is very difficult to determine.

Although the large corporations covered wider markets and geographical areas they lacked the economic discipline and could no longer compete successfully against smaller, foreign companies. The growing inefficiencies of these giant corporations also affected their suppliers and customers. Most of America's declining giants failed to reform themselves as they faced increasing competition from abroad.

The inability of the U.S. to create major new competitors or breaking up large firms in their mature industries left them with only two options. They are:

a) Foreign competitors take over, with some resultant loss of U.S. economic welfare.

b) If no foreign competition appears, the U.S. industry goes into uncontested decline, imposing the costs of its inefficiency on the American economy and population.

The result has usually been a combination of both. Since the 1970's the failure to adjust has eventually led to crises, downsizings, bankruptcies or acquisitions in the large U.S. companies. The companies' management generally resisted change as long as they could, often through political activities, and consequently suffered even more severely when reality could no longer be denied. These costs were added to the already huge damages of the financial services.

The executives of these large corporations reduced their high-cost local workers by outsourcing jobs to low paid workers in Asia. Although the companies achieved higher efficiency it reduced local employment, lowered education skills of its people and losing its attraction for high technology activities.

Since the late 1970's America's major industries discovered and began exploiting a critical weakness in the U.S. national system to escape competitive discipline. They discovered that buying people off was much easier than doing their job properly. They proved that the American politicians, academics, regulators, auditors were highly corruptible and they were able to weaken regulations, enforcement, penalties for violations, and virtually eliminated any risk of criminal prosecution.

Americans have suffered under the same three things as people under a corrupt dictatorship when the system is rigged and the ordinary citizens are powerless. First, the worst people rise to the top who behave appallingly and they wreak havoc. Second, people who could make productive contributions to society are prone to become destructive, because corruption is far more lucrative than honest work. Thirdly everyone else pay, both economically and emotionally; people become cynical, selfish, and fatalistic.

Economics need a balance between the role of markets and the role of the government. In the past twenty-five years, America lost that balance, and it pushed its unbalanced perspective on countries around the world.

The American financial system has been repeatedly been rescued by the government proving that their economic system hadn't been working so well for most of its citizens. Somebody was doing well, but it was not the average American.

American consumers, once the envy of the world, face an uncertain, debt-laden future, while more than 30 million Chinese leap into the ranks of the middle class every year. This is made worse by financial companies that constantly reallocate capital away from mature developed economies, where giant debt burdens will restrain growth for years to come.

The communist creed: from each according to his ability, to each according to his need. This was changed by the moneylenders to read: From each according to his gullibility, to each according to his greed.

The Americans are beginning to conclude that:

The economy is in worse shape than the government says it is.

Consumers are getting less value for their money than previously and instead of rising, their standard of living is actually eroding.

Markets once thought to be fair are being secretly manipulated by government to the detriment of the average citizen.

The police and military are spying on and threatening them in seemingly-unconstitutional ways.

Banks and other corporations are using their dominance of the financial system to commit increasingly blatant and far-reaching fraud.

The tallest buildings, biggest dams, largest-selling movies, and the most advanced cell phones are all being made/built outside America, making their decline a reality.

American economy could become number two in the world as early as 2016. The world will not end when America becomes number two.

Senior military and intelligence officials have now come to the realization that America's unique military predominance can only be maintained with an equally unique and predominant role of the dollar. If the dollar falls, America's national security falls with it.

What are the solutions?

America need to stop bailouts, restructure its debt, reduce government spending, stop borrowing, increase interest rates, and reduce subsidies. The citizens need to reduce their debt and start saving.

14. Japan

In the nineteenth century Japan like China was under absolute rule and they were both poor nations. The Tokugawa family took over in 1600 and ruled over a feudal system that also banned international trade.

During the Japanese Meiji Revolution of 1868 the Japanese warlords were overthrown and a modern central government was formed. The new government abolished the ownership of Japan's land by the feudal samurai nobles and returned it to the nation, paying the nobles a sum of money in return.

The Bank of Japan was founded on October 10, 1882 and functioned as a typical central bank, i.e. for the benefit of private banks to the detriment of the public interest.

Japan commenced in 1932 to reorganise the Bank of Japan into a state bank for the accomplishment of national interest. The reform was completed in 1942 when the Bank of Japan was remodelled on Germany's Reichsbank Act of January 1939. The conversion from a central to state banking methodology produced results which were both swift and sustained once the shackles of usury had been removed.

Japan became the first nation in Asia to found its own independent state bank. The bank issued fiat money which was used to pay the samurai nobles. The nobles were then encouraged to deposit their money in the state bank and put it to work creating new industries.

This was a state-guided market system where the state determines the priorities and hires private enterprise to carry it out. The model overcame the defects of the communist system which put ownership and control in the hands of the state.

When Japan went off the gold standard in 1931 they devalued the yen by 60 percent against the dollar to increase export. Japan was the first non-Western country to accelerate into industrialization.

During the 1931-41 period manufacturing output and industrial production increased by 140% and 136% respectively, while national income and Gross National Product were up by 241% and 259% respectively. These remarkable increases exceeded by a wide margin the economic growth of the rest of the industrialised world.

From July 1939 relations with America rapidly deteriorated when US unilaterally cancelled the Treaty of Commerce of 1911 and restricted Japan's ability to import essential raw materials. During 1941 all Japanese assets in England, Holland and America were frozen, while President F.D. Roosevelt closed the Panama Canal to all Japanese shipping, and a rubber and oil embargo was enforced. Without oil Japan could not survive. Although Japan tried with diplomatic negotiation US did not budge.

By 1941 Japan had been cut from 75% of her normal trade by the Allied blockade saw no other option but to attack America to maintain her prosperity and to secure her existence as a sovereign nation.

The defeat of Japan enabled the Detroit bankers to restructure the Japanese banking system to make it compliant with the norms of the international bankers i.e. usury. The Japanese however, retained a measure of control over their banking and monetary policy.

During the long post-war boom, the Japanese economy had depended on the expansion of exports. It not only relied on the rapid growth of world export markets but the growing shares of that market, especially the U.S.

The state intervened between manufacturing corporations, banks investors and consumers to increase investment growth and exports while keeping household consumption and imports low. The government did this by tight control of credit markets, keeping interest rates low for local manufacturers, protecting capital markets from foreign penetration, while depriving consumers of credit. The consumers were thus forced to save to buy their big ticket items.

The government intervention caused that during the 1970's when most countries experienced high inflation rates Japan had relatively mild inflation due to the restraint of its monetary policies by the Bank of Japan.

The Japanese state-guided market system was so effective and efficient that by the end of the 1980s, Japan was regarded as the leading economic and banking power in the world.

Things You Should Know

With the Plaza Accord of 1985 things changed, the U.S dollar went into a steep decline which caused a sharp ascent for both the yen and the mark. The pressure was lifted from the U.S. manufactures and shifted to their competitors in Japan and Germany.

In April 1988 the ministry of Finance was forced by law to yield to the independence bank of Japan. Since that time the Bank of Japan has functioned as a typical Rothschild controlled central bank, which seldom preforms its duties in the best interests of the Japanese people.

The Japanese government ran large budget deficits to increase economic growth and to finance World War II. Soon after the war the country was effectively able to inflate its way out of its debt.

The manufacturing economy of Japan faced over-capacity and over-production problems in the international economy. The rise in their currency and the relative fast wage growth reduced their competitiveness which led to reduced profit rates and capital accumulation.

They responded by reorienting production, trade and finance to East Asia for its cheaper labour and better exchange rates. This enabled Japanese corporations to penetrate indirectly into the U.S. market while also proving access to the fast-growing markets of Asia itself. Japanese banks supplied huge loans to Japanese corporations initiating operations in East Asia, as well as to East Asian corporations.

During the first half of the 1990s, manufacturing investment in East Asia recorded an average profit to sales ratio that almost tripled that in Japan. By 1994 the Japanese economy emerged from its recession but was once again interrupted by the strong rise of the yen. Weary of the continuous dollar devaluation the Japanese investors stayed away from U.S assets.

With the Mexican peso crisis in late 1994 there was a new run on the dollar and by April 1995 the yen had reached its highest level in history, at 79 yen to the U.S.$. Manufacturing investment to East Asia surged in response to yen appreciation until overseas production began to have a net negative effect on domestic production and employment.

Japanese imports accelerated and became a major drag on the growth of GDP while the local manufacturing economy freezing up, threatened a new recession and a flight of Japanese capital from the U.S.

Japan's citizens have done what all increasingly urban and affluent societies do: They have fewer children because the cost of raising them goes up in an increasingly urban society. It is simply a natural human impulse to have fewer kids and educate them better.

Focusing on individual goals however may not always be good for collective and long-term economic growth.

Japan's banking dominance is the product of an ageing population with very high private savings, which continue to earn returns higher than the rate of economic growth. The model also proved highly successful in the "Tiger" economics. East Asia was built up with Japanese state development aid.

However, the Tiger economics were a major embarrassment to the IMF free-market model which threatened their system of debt-based money and IMF loans. Japan was forced by Washington to cut their interest rates to a low 2.5%.

The result was a flood of "cheap" money that was turned into quick gains on the rising Tokyo stock market, producing an enormous stock market bubble. Many Japanese investors embarked upon a speculative frenzy aimed at the profitable buying and selling of real estate in the metropolitan areas of Japan. The local banks met the 'investment' demand, creating a dramatic increase in metropolitan property prices.

When the Japanese government tried to deflate the bubble by raising interest rates, the Wall Street bankers went on the attack, using their derivatives to sell the market short and bring it crashing down. The Japanese economy suffered severely as the Japanese stocks had lost nearly $5 trillion in paper value within months.

By the 1990s the Japanese banking system had become overloaded with bad loans after a property collapse, sparking a crisis. The largest banks were desperate to find ways to reduce their risk. The Japanese government bailed out the banks which caused it in turn to go into massive debt.

The strategy worked because Japan's financial sector did not collapse but disaster avoidance came at a price as the companies could not function without continued infusion of public money. One stimulus program followed another, ballooning Japan's public debt.

Persistent deflation is caused by a lack of demand as people are holding onto their money as prices continue to fall which caused GDP to barely increase while government debt increased. The interest rates are so low that banks had no incentive to lend money out and with the very low returns on investment in Japan people did not want to borrow either.

To increase lending and the velocity of money the Bank of Japan is struggling while they are doing all the wrong things at the wrong times to stimulate the economy.

Japan relied on nuclear power but when the earthquake hit the Japanese coast in 2011 it severely damaged their nuclear plant. They had to switch overnight and import very expensive gas, coal, and oil.

A year later the trade account showed its first deficit since 1980. For an aging country the numbers were disastrous. Since 2012 the sales of adult diapers surpassed sales of baby diapers. And for the third year in a row the number of people in Japan has dropped and the number of elderly relative to other age groups is growing fast.

The country has a high government debt and almost all that debt is held by Japanese individuals and institutions. Japan is in a liquidity trap where some of the usual rules of economics don't apply. Large budget deficits don't drive up interest rates; printing money is not inflationary; and cutting government spending has an exaggerated impact on the economy.

Since 2012 the new Prime Minister, Shinzo Abe is on a massive money printing spree to haul the economy out of a long period of economic stagnation and mild deflation, by weakening the currency, create inflation and finance large-scale government spending.

The low value of the yen causes companies in Asia and Europe to drop their prices to compete with the Japanese firms. The pressure on central banks world-wide is even bigger to respond to the Japanese devaluing their yen.

In Japan and Europe the level of government debt has gone up as the economy has stagnated and even contracted. Japan's trade deficit surged nearly 70 per cent to a record $156 billion in the last fiscal year as exports failed to keep pace with surging costs for imported oil and gas.

Japan had a stock peak in the late 1989 and its demographic peak in late 1996. As its population keeps aging, the QE stimulus is only achieving the growing of government debt while the economy stays stagnant.

Although Japan has been doing QE or money injections and running massive fiscal deficits for seventeen years now, its economy has continued to fall back into recession and its stock market has continue to fall to new lows or near new lows after each stimulus-led rally.

Since the 1990's the Japanese economy has been running contrary to those of most developed countries. This is due to its falling demographic trends while America and Europe were experiencing strong trends.

15. China

For most of us China has always been a country of tall tales and mystical sayings, an appeal to the imagination. From Marco Polo's fascinating stories to Mao's Little Red Book we have impressions of an alluring, mysterious, inaccessible eastern country, reflected in our own prejudices and preconceptions rather than the realities of China.

We still knew very little of China due to our apprehension, and preconceptions, of what we read about in the biased media that influence perceptions. But we plunge straight in tendering advice without obtaining enough information

China has an old and complex culture, yet our view of it is simple. After nearly half a century Westerners are less restricted in going to China, travelling within, talking, and listening to the citizens. The country is now more open to the world maybe not so much of an upsurge of Westernised capitalism but as a golden age of reformed socialism.

Chinese people are now perceived as the

kind you would most like your children to go to school with, the least likely to cause trouble, although they hardly make any attempt at assimilation. The Chinese are not only aware of their difference they assert their right to it.

The Chinese culture is one of the world's oldest cultures with customs and traditions varying greatly between provinces, cities and even towns. There are 56 officially recognised ethnic groups in China.

Since the Three Sovereigns and Five Emperors period, some form of Chinese monarch has been the main ruler above all. Different periods of history have different names for the various positions within society. Conceptually each imperial or feudal period are similar, with the government and military officials ranking high in the hierarchy, and the rest of the population under regular Chinese laws. From the late Zhou Dynasty onwards, traditional Chinese society was organised into a hierarchical system of socio-economic classes known as the four occupations.

Since the Song Dynasty the distinctions between the groups became blurred. From the Sui Dynasty educated candidates prepared for the imperial examinations which drafted exam candidates into government. Most social values are derived from Confucianism, Buddhism and Taoism. For much of the eighteenth century China flourished and was admired for their

Eastern wisdom, fine poetry and profound philosophy.

By 1949 continuous foreign invasions, frequent revolutions, and civil wars had left the country with a fragile economy and little infrastructure. Since the formation of the People's Republic in 1949, an enormous effort was made towards creating economic growth and entirely new industries were created. Tight control of the budget and money supply reduced inflation by the end of 1950. The campaigns which followed were anti-capitalism and capitalists were severely punished.

The government nationalised the country's banking system and brought all currency and credit under a centralised system; they also brought the bulk of China's industry and commerce under their direct control. With the land reform they confiscated private land and redistributed it to the peasant households.

In 1958 Mao tried to push China's economy to new heights and farmers were reorganised into enormous communes where people were assigned in military fashion to specific tasks. They were told to stop relying on the family and adopt a system of communal kitchens, mess halls and nurseries. Crime and disorder was low and one could walk the streets in safety at midnight.

Wages were calculated along the

communist principle of "From each according to his ability, to each according to his need", and sideline production was banned as the beginning stage of capitalism. All Chinese citizens were urged to boost the country's steel production by establishing "backyard" steel furnaces to help overtake the west.

This all back-fired and China was gripped by a devastating famine. Tens of millions of Chinese suffered in silence.

For the next several years China experienced a period of relative stability until 1966, when Mao proclaimed a Cultural Revolution and the country descended into anarchy. All he achieved under his rule was a nation congealed into a single homogenous mass, a robot army who despised the West. The individual had no meaning in this culture the human personality was reduced to nothing.

Prior to 1978 almost all enterprises were owned by the state. At the top of each sector was the State-owned Enterprises (SOE's) reporting to the government. Below these were the other enterprises reporting to provincial, municipal or country authorities. There were no private enterprises. The SOE's were typically large industrial firms which provided housing, day-care, education and health care for their workers and families.

Reforms began in the 1980's and the leaders put their pragmatic policies to work to bring China back from the devastating conditions that the Cultural Revolution had caused. China made major reforms to its economy as they introduced aspects of capitalism; raising personal income and consumption to increase productivity. Private enterprises were allowed but limited to seven employees.

For economic growth China permitted foreign direct investment in certain areas along the coast. They added incentives to attract foreign capital such as reduced taxes, better infrastructure and legal aspects.

Reform took off in the countryside by breaking up the communes established by Mao and replacing them with a complicated system of leases but the land remained state owned. The farmers were allowed to sell any surplus they produced and within a decade grain production had grown by 30% and the production of cotton, sugarcane tobacco and fruit had doubled.

The history of 20th century China is one of experimentation with new systems of social, political, and economic organisation that would allow for the reintegration of the nation in the wake of dynastic collapse.

André Klopper

Rising from the Maoist ashes, the Chinese raced with their economic liberation to modernize industries to meet the basic needs of the people and to fight against poverty. The Chinese entrepreneurs and Chinese energies have also helped keep America's inflation and interest rates down with little improvements to their own human rights.

There is an underlying contradiction-the idea that you can have economic without political freedom. China has become a wealthier and in some respects freer country and there are compromises of every description, but for the foreseeable future central conflict will stay.

China's progression towards democracy depends on the growing middle class who will demand it. Within decades an almost non existing middle class grew to several million people who are enjoying a sharp rise in living standards and are more relaxed and informed.

However not all Chinese are benefiting from the best of times the country has enjoyed for over a century. The livelihoods of the rural population are lagging behind and hundreds of millions are driven to roam the country in search of work.

China has sped up and everyone is impatient. The wonder of the modern Chinese world is not so much its industrial productivity as the revival of its spiritually dead people. Their resurrection within decades into a dynamic and increasingly diversified society is a triumph of human nature. With hope, ingenuity and determination they have succeeded.

The relationship between Chinese workers and their employers is better balanced due to unplanned changes which is good for workers' rights but challenge the state-designed system.

An expanding economy run by a corrupt and authoritarian communist party is unsustainable. China with its one-party state finds itself isolated amongst the democratic world which still remains imperfect. As the country roars unsteadily ahead a larger middle class will emerge which will demand their rights and democracy will follow, as day follows night.

Prime Minister, Wen Jiabao once said, 'democracy is a value pursued by all mankind and a fruit of civilization created by mankind. However, in different historical stages and different countries democracy is achieved through different forms and in different ways.'

Currently about 50 million people of Chinese decent live outside China who are proud to belong to one of the world's most prosperous powers. Their patriotism has increased over the last decades. China's aggressive global strategy together with their large funds produced by their trade surplus with the West provides the country with more options. China is gaining power and confidence.

China went through different cultures at different stages of development to combine their autocratic traditions with twenty-first century capitalism. A system they belatedly adopted because only capitalism can produce sufficient wealth to satisfy popular demands, legitimating their power, and make their country strong. They understand that a fuller democracy is their ultimate goal. They want to keep discipline society and will not allow disorder among the people.

The Chinese government is working very hard to ensure no alternative party can come into power. Their history makes it plausible to speculate that, with or without democracy there will be limits to political liberties.

Some observers believe China needs an alternative path to sustained economic growth, one under authoritarianism rather than inclusive economic and political institutions, they are wrong. Chinese growth is likely to come to an end when China reaches the standards of living level of a middle-income country if the Chinese Communist Party maintains their tight grip on power. The reason is no true innovations will occur and the spectacular growth rates will slowly evaporate.

Things You Should Know

The Chinese leaders have confidence in themselves and their future, for good reason, and with millennia of civilization behind them are feeling a bit superior. We can therefore assume that a working democracy is unlikely to be accomplished within a short period. But it can easily slip into reverse or switch to a more rampant capitalism, anything is possible.

There is no prospect of any mass uprising soon, for the Chinese don't fret over the absence of full democracy as they are content with fuller bellies than any other generation before them in the last sixty years.

China's economic success was dependent on exporting cheaply to the United States. To do so, they needed not only to hold wages down, but also to keep their currency low. This entailed buying billions of dollars. While the Chinese did the savings the Americans did the spending. The cheap Chinese imports enable the Americans to keep their inflation low.

The problem with China's growth and investment boom is so extreme that it is unsustainable and unbalanced. While China are building bridges, factories, and ports their household consumption has not been keeping pace with infrastructure investment.

With this huge industrialisation and urbanisation process China became the biggest buyer of commodities in the world of copper, iron ore, aluminium coal, and cement. China has built too much, too quickly.

As China's economy rebalances towards a much more sustainable form of growth the country will need a reduced quantity of commodities which will lead to a drop in prices.

But if the Chinese government moves too slowly to restrict credit and let inflation gain too much, people's cost of living would rise and the Chinese firms would rapidly lose competitiveness. On the other hand if the central bank tightened monetary conditions too fast, job growth would slow. Both scenarios raise the prospect of civil unrest of which the authorities are downright paranoid.

The enormous U.S. financial imbalances hangs like a dark cloud over the U.S. and the world economy-the overvalued stock market, the huge U.S. current account balances, massive U.S. overseas debt and the record breaking U.S. private sector deficits.

All the above and the over-capacity of the U.S. manufacturing and a deflation of their stock market would propel the country towards a serious recession and in the process detonate further recessions all across the rest of the world.

Today the image of Beijing is a city under a

lowering cloud of pollution as an ash-grey pall covers everything. The ingredients are factory effluent, the smoke of coal power stations, car exhaust fumes, and the dust of building constructions. The poison they produce goes for your throat and is blanking out the sun.

Many of the rivers have a soupy appearance, fouled by waste water or industrial effluent. Half of China's waterways are so badly affected they can no longer be used for irrigation, let alone drinking water.

Hugely expanded coastal cities spill half their wastewater directly into the sea, and the number and extent of coastal fish die-offs have risen dramatically. So the Chinese fishermen venture further, with the result that in the China Sea many species face complete extinction.

The Chinese are feeling their way across a bridgeless river with no precedents to guide them as to how their country should be governed in the post-Mao era. They are trying to kerb pollution and corruption while modernizing the country and get their government in sync with international trends.

China is a big place and the road to liberty could be long and perilous.

André Klopper

16. Asia & Australasia: The Dynamic Region

Since the 1990's Japan, Korea, Taiwan, China, Malaysia, Indonesia and Thailand have expanded at least 7 per cent a year growth until the Asian financial crises took hold. Malaysia Indonesia and Thailand were knocked off course; Japan a mature economy faced a new set of problems while Korea, Taiwan, China quickly recovered from it.

There is a huge difference between the productivity of owner-farmer land and that of tenanted land. The landlords were exploiting the peasantry who were toiling the land throughout the whole year knowing neither warmth nor full stomachs.

With China, Japan, Korea and Taiwan the governments began their reform by dividing the agricultural land equally among the farming population backed by training and support services. This resulted in huge increases in their agriculture production with intensive labour. The increase in agriculture output led to increased surplus which implies more savings which were used to finance industrial investment.

These countries began their industrialisation with an overwhelming rural population. These rural areas were home to many new manufacturing enterprises and produced many industrial entrepreneurs. Industries increased their output by manufacturing products to satisfy the needs of the household farming population.

Countries, however, cannot sustain growth on agriculture alone. Returns from land reform and other agriculture begin to taper off after only a decade or so, and emerging economies have to go into another phase of development. That phase has historically revolved around manufacturing. Manufacturing is important as un-skilled and semi-skilled labourers can develop further, and is also more freely traded than services.

Manufacturing allows for trade and trade is essential to rapid economic development. Through it poor countries learn productive skills from more advanced economies and acquire new technologies. Developing countries' manufacturing doesn't have to be as efficient as it is in advanced economic countries as they can use highly motivated, cut price, fresh-off-the-farm labourers and obtain government assistance.

The interest of national development and business has to be forcibly aligned in order to succeed. The capacity to export told politicians what worked and what didn't and they responded accordingly with tax breaks and subsidies. The successful countries did not so much pick winners as weed out losers. The lack of export discipline causes manufacturing exports to fail.

North East Asian countries did not reinvent the wheel; they copied examples of successful economic modernisation in the United States and Europe. Manufacturing policy was copied from the example of Germany which provided Meiji Japan with a case study of successful industrialisation.

From the 1950's Japanese manufacturing and mining output increased more than tenfold in only two decades. Many people thought the country had discovered a new and unbeatable form of economic management; Japan had merely rediscovered old ideas and built on earlier German refinements thereof. From Japan, ideas spread to Korea, Taiwan and China.

The final, essential modification to successful industrialisation is the policy of a subsidy system that forces big business to behave in the interest of national development, and to export. This reduces cartels exploiting smaller companies and consumers while they prevent price cutting.

Australia:

Australia is a large English speaking

country with plenty of natural resources. The Australians had to fight to obtain inclusive institutions. Once these were in place, Australia launched its own process of economic growth. The country industrialised and grew rapidly due to innovation and new technologies. Australia has a strong export market with Asia and has a huge supply of natural gas.

Although Australia's overall debt as a proportion of GDP remains at comparatively low levels of 12.5% the government debt rose from A$58 billion in 2007 to A$300 billion in 2014. This is causing a "billion dollars a month" interest.

The debt as a proportion of GDP can be a bit misleading as the governments income is not the entire GDP of the country. A more meaningful figure is the debt as a proportion of government revenue which is about 54%

If a banking crash occurs the big international City of London Corporation banks are planning to place Australian and New Zealand banks into statutory management and confiscate most people's savings. This will happen overnight when they plan to wipe out excess liquidity in the system.

By crashing the system, and largely using depositor's funds to fund the bank's losses, the bank's secured creditors can take over all the assets in both countries.

The International Monetary Fund (IMF) recommended that advanced economies with high debts, escalate income by increasing consumption and inheritance taxes, culminating in imposing a one-off "wealth levy." The capital levy- a one-off tax on private wealth, as an exceptional measure to restore debt sustainability. The tax rates needed to bring down public debt to pre-crisis levels.

China:

China has established itself as the undisputed manufacturing centre of the world, and it seemed to be on a mission to produce every fabricated item the world consumes. What first began with a focus on low-wage labour-intensive industries grew to include almost the full range of consumer electronics.

China doesn't have enough food to feed its growing urban labour force, or enough base metals to supply its manufacturing companies. The country has to obtain these from elsewhere. Trade with Africa grew 33 percent each year since 2000 to obtain the natural resources needed.

The Chinese had won favour with the African governments by improving the infrastructure to make resource extraction and shipment easier. They also engaged in public works projects importing tens of thousands Chinese labourers to build airports, toll roads, gas pipelines and housing projects. China as a trading partner is offering the continent a sense of hope that Western aid has long failed to provide.

All is not as positive in the Kenyan environment organizations reported an alarming pickup in the ivory trade which they associated with the arrival of Chinese poachers. The influx of Chinese in some areas took jobs from the locals which resulted in riots against the Chinese communities.

China's capacity for many clean energy products exceeded that of other countries while their bullet train became the world's fastest passenger train in service. Much of this spectacular advancement was possible because of efficiencies provided by China's overwhelming pool of low-cost and highly productive labour.

America faced an unrelenting competitive challenge with their high labour costs and had to move their own production or let foreign suppliers do the work for them.

Hong Kong:

Hong Kong is a model of capitalism, has low taxes and low regulation, making it the corporate Mecca of Asia. The Hong Kong Stock

Exchange is the fifth largest in the world.

New Zealand:

New Zealand is a small agricultural nation with great potential that is slowly shifting into manufacturing. It is a strong social welfare state. The country is pursuing free-trade agreements around the globe as its economy had become one of the most deregulated in the world.

After the Napoleonic wars, Britain was heavily indebted with high unemployment and a few rich people looking for investment and speculation. The New Zealand Association was formed in 1838 to make money. It began selling land in New Zealand before it acquired a single acre of land.

Just ahead of the first shiploads of emigrants a few Maori chiefs were given presents for a million acres of land. By 1850 when the company surrendered its charter to the Crown they had not given legal title to one of the twelve thousand people who had immigrated to New Zealand.

In 1856 the colonist in their first Parliament had to raise a £200,000 loan to extinguish the company's claim on the colony.

It was the beginning of the public debt of New Zealand. Although the colonists found ways to acquire land at low prices they were quickly indebted with high interest rates to the banks. The Colonists could be bankrupted at any moment by their bankers quietly calling up their loans.

In 1860 the Maori war broke out as a consequence of the Government taking possession of land which the Maoris contended they had not sold to the Crown. A large area of land was confiscated after the war which was offered at public auction.

Within a few years of its establishment about half of the banking in New Zealand was done by the Bank of New Zealand and had the colony farmers in debt. This gave the bank owners enough power to manipulate the politics in Parliament and control the media.

When Mr Vogel convinced the colony to borrow ten million over a period of ten years for improving infrastructure in 1870, the population of a quarter of a million was already laden with eight million of Government debt. At the end of the ten years twenty million had been borrowed and only two thirds of the work was completed. Since then the country has simply been borrowing money to pay the interest on what it was owing before. The public debt had been compounding, and rose from about £30 million in 1885 to NZ$70,814,000,000 on the 30 April 2014.

To place the NZ$70 billion in perspective,

during 2013 the crown revenue and expenses were just over NZ$60 billion each, not enough surplus to even cover the interest rate payments.

Both the National and Labour parties are committed to maintaining the welfare state and the associated belief in a regulated economy. Decades of investment misdirected towards money-lending and speculation rather than in the construction of real industrial and social assets and the supporting infrastructure had taken their toll.

17. The Philippines & Sri Lanka

Philippines:

The Cojuangcos of the Philippines originally built up their agricultural holdings in Tarlac in the nineteenth century through agricultural usury. The rich landlords in the Philippines avoided land reforms and are still controlling the majority of farmlands with going wages for a farm labourer of U.S.$2.60 a day. The periodic unrest born of poverty has affected the Philippines for centuries.

Ferdinand Marcos declared martial law in 1972 promising a New Society and land reform. His limited land reform was largely targeted at property belonging to his political enemies. When his successor Cory Aquino's vast family estate was sought under the new reform law she obtained permission to avoid the radical reform on their property. By doing this she made it abundantly clear that radical reform under people power is not going to happen.

Although the Philippine government claims that the implementation of the Comprehensive Agrarain reform Law has met most of its national targets. It has not, for today an estimated 8.5 million of the 11.2 million rural workers are landless. Where land reform did take place it was without complicated infrastructure to deliver fertilisers and seeds, leaving small farms to struggle. Therefore the majority of people in the countryside live in poverty.

Land reform has been overseen by corrupt government bureaucrats between owners and tenants. Sometimes so unfair the process involved transfer of wealth from poor to rich.

In the Negros area lives one of the Philippines' richest businessmen, Eduardo 'Danding' Cojuangco. He is the biggest landowner in the area running the coconut trading monopoly while the Benedicto family run the sugar market monopoly. The rich landowners ensure the new small farmers fail by charging them exorbitant rates.

The most powerful people of the world travelled all over the Third World because that was where the commodities were. Marcos's number one guy Don-ding Corleone Cojuangco had a monopoly on bananas and beer in the Philippines. Controlling commodities was how the dictators stayed in power. By dealing with these dictators the most powerful people stayed in power at the expense of the populace working in these controlled commodity industries.

Despite the insistence of the rich landlords that farming can only be competitive on large farms their yields are far lower than in China and Taiwan. In fact in the Philippines, farming remains grotesquely inefficient.

Sri Lanka:

Sri Lanka became independent in 1948. The small island is smaller than Scotland but has four times its population, is well positioned in the great sea routes of the Indian Ocean and had benefited from railways, roads and administration of British colonialism. It was predicted that the country would become an economic powerhouse in Asia trumping Singapore, South Korea and even Japan.

The country has however spawned governments that use the familiar language of liberal democrats while deploying death squads to kill journalists, students and political opponents. Since 1972, the independence of the country's police force and judicial institutions has been increasingly degraded to serve the predilections of its leaders.

Its parliament today is little more than a small group of oppositionists overwhelmed by a gaggle of provincial potentates and party sycophants, who gather to rubber-stamp the wishes of the country's president and his family, in return for the spoils of government.

Its once free press has been largely cowed into serving the dominant ideology of politicised Buddhism. In 2008, the island could fairly be called one of the most dangerous places in the world to be a journalist or humanitarian worker, between 2006 and 2008 dozens died just doing their jobs.

The nation bred a liberation group, the Tamil Tigers who thought appalling violence through armed conflict was the only option to topple the oppressive regime. The Tamil Tigers had established a vast network of finance and fund-raising in Tamil communities throughout the world, mustered a fleet of merchant ships and imported the arms, machinery and knowledge that is required to build an army, special forces capability and even an air force.

During the war a huge number of civilians were killed by government forces as they worked their way across the Tamil Tiger controlled territory. These war crimes were used in solving civil conflict but only lead to more wars.

The depth of hatred by conflicting identities is palpable in Sri Lanka, but it only shows that the divide between orderly, law-abiding societies and those that descend into a collective madness governed by hatred is a thin one. Civilisation, with all its supreme accomplishments, is a fragile veneer that must be constantly repaired.

We cannot discuss grand ideologies, the greed and brutality of politicians, murderous clerics, the culpability of leadership, ethnic cleansing, murder and love between neighbours or the experimentation with different political systems without looking within our own examples, and to the resuscitation of our own societies. The lesson of Sri Lanka is that we must always be sentinel to the weakness in our human design.

18. Singapore

Singapore a 25km by 40km island was established as a major trading centre in 1819 by British colonist Stamford Raffles. Since then the island has had a rich and varied history. Although the country had over 500 factories in the 1950s the people experienced a typical Third World status with a per capita income the same as Ghana. They had no flush toilets, some malnutrition, ethnic riots, and most important of all, no sense of hope for the future.

By August 1965 when Singapore separated from Malaysia the country was the natural convergence point for about 50 maritime nations and more than 200 shipping lanes. Despite its limited land area (639 sq km) inhabited by two million people, Singapore had a sizeable agriculture sector, which made it largely self-sufficient in food production. Many Singaporeans grew their own food in small backyard plots, and even by 1969 Singapore still produced enough to meet all of its pork, poultry, egg, and fish needs.

Singapore's greatest asset is its people. Even in 1965, they had one of Asia's most educated and literate populations, capable and hardworking although more than half the population lived in slums. To control population growth large families lost child tax credits and priority access to subsidized housing.

Since Lee Kuan Yew became prime minister in 1959 he has always displayed a ruthless intolerance for inefficiency and incompetence, and has stamped this attitude on the Singaporean consciousness. "Striving for

Excellence" is one of the more abiding slogans of Singapore Inc.

Soon after gaining independence, the Prime Minister Lee Kuan Yew devised a blueprint for developing Singapore, opting for four basic strategies to assure its survival; rapid industrialisation, export-based development, the state to operate strategic industries that foreign or private sectors could not, and the development of financial services.

Singapore has the freest economy in the world with a huge trade surplus due to its manufacturing exports to China, Australia and India.

Singapore's high growth rates since then have enhanced its glowing global reputation. From the 1980s as Singapore's reputation thrived, increasing numbers of foreign political and business leaders visited the city-state to learn the secrets of its success.

When the travellers arrive at the incredible Changi airport they are amazed when they are whisked by taxi through the island's skyscraper landscape and can observe the cleanliness and efficiency of the country.

They are however, totally unaware of *Kiasuism*, a cluster of values, beliefs and attitudes which significantly determine Singaporeans behaviour. *Kiasu* is a Chines word which means "fear of missing out". Key features of the *kiasu* personality are greed, materialism, selfishness, getting something for nothing, insensitivity to others' feelings, taking advantage of other people and a deep fear of failure. It is an awful social disease of self-centred disregard for community that will infect wherever allowed to and retard the republic's progress towards a cultured society.

19. Europe

Although Europe was constantly in a state of war it has been dominating the globe for the last six centuries. After World War I during the League of Nations in 1929 Gustav Stresemann asked for a European currency.

In December 1969 the European Commission set out the need for greater co-ordination of economic policies and monetary coordination in the Hague. On 14th June 1988 in Hanover the European Council began to outline monetary co-operation by a fully monetary union with a central bank; however the British Prime Minister Margaret Thatcher opposed it.

Four years later Europe agreed to create a single currency without participation of the United Kingdom. The goal became a reality when the euro came into existence on the 1st January 1999. In 2002 the notes and coins began to circulate and it rapidly took over from the former national currencies and slowly expanded behind the rest of the EU.

The primary appeal of the single currency is that it makes intra-zone trade much easier; the costs and revenues of business in different countries are in the same currency. The Germans do not have to worry that when selling things to countries within Europe that the other country's currency could depreciate. Tourists travelling across Europe do not have the hassle or expense of changing currencies every time they cross a border.

The smaller countries hitched a ride on the reputation of the German Deutschmark, one of the world's strongest currencies in the second half of the twentieth century. In the early days of the euro, this seemed to be nothing but a benefit to the peripheral countries. Their borrowing cost fell, converging with those of Germany, while avoiding the exchange rate fluctuations that had marked the 1970s and early 1990s.

The Europeans however were running the monetary policy of Germany without the Germans' drive for thrift or competitive industry. The result was either credit-fuelled construction booms (Ireland and Spain) or repeated trade deficits (Greece and Portugal).

The euro is now used by 28 member states of the European Union with a population of 334 million people. The euro is the second largest reserve currency as well as the second most traded currency in the world after the United States dollar.

Following the U.S. financial crisis in 2008, fears of a sovereign debt crisis developed in 2009 among fiscally conservative investors concerning some European states. As these countries struggle to rescue their banking sectors, and cope with the rising debt burden, the future of the euro has been called into question.

A break up in the European monetary union could spell global financial disaster. There would be a flood of defaults and bankruptcies, giant losses for the world's banks and quite possibly a breakdown in the global trade and payment systems, a prospect made more likely because of the disproportionate role that European banks play in financing the world's exporters and importers. The European banks are three times more invested in emerging markets than the U.S. banks.

A complete crisis would reverberate around the world. The extent of the damage would depend on whether there is a partial or full break up in the euro, but even if only Greece were to leave, the ramifications would be profoundly painful and far-reaching.

André Klopper

Government leaders and the ECB know that a break up would be suicidal hence the widely held view is that they would do everything possible to stay united. However, there is no guarantee that the pressures created by the regions internal imbalances won't reach breaking point.

The euro can be saved only if the rest of the world believes that it can be saved. If their creditors believe that it is doomed, the euro will collapse. To save the euro, Europe must learn to work more effectively with the rest of the world.

Public trust is the wild card in all this. Already citizens' confidence in the euro financial system is at an all-time low and to a large extent because they perceive that the cost of saving the euro are not being shared fairly by those who profited before the crisis, including the bankers.

The lifestyle cutbacks that the Europeans are enduring will only become more severe as their economies shrink, driving up their governments' debt loads and their interest rates.

Many Europeans are already angry because the EU and the IMF had placed severe conditions on their funding of the euro governments and Japan and China demanded trade concessions in return for investing their reserves in the euro zone bonds.

Europe remains dangerously fragmented, both politically and economically, with the EU seemingly incapable of coherent action. The economies remain weak, with high unemployment and low growth despite continued deficit spending. The sovereign debt problems of Greece, Portugal, Ireland, Italy and Spain are unsustainable and will likely trigger another crisis. The loans these countries have received do not solve anything as their debts are too great.

The Euro governments who are asking their people to give up their sovereignty are facing a grave test of its legitimacy. Europe is destined for a lengthy, painful adjustment to a period of much slower growth, high unemployment, and ongoing asset deflation. The social unrest could become unbearable and cause the euro to collapse.

20. The Politicians

Three thousand years ago, the Greek philosopher Plato argued that the best form of government is one in which a "philosopher king" employs absolute power to create and maintain a just society. A strong leader gets things done, so according to this line of thought the key to success is to find the right person and turn them loose to make the system work.

History has shown the philosopher king to be one of those intriguing ideals that, when attempted in the real world, always and everywhere falls prey to human nature. Power, it has by now been established beyond all doubt, corrupts. Good, well-meaning leaders become demagogues who put pride and ideas of 'legacy' above the welfare of citizens. Demagogues become corrupt, feathering their own nests by looting their subjects' wealth.

Question: In today's world, which politician would survive the longest, the one telling the truth or the one telling his voters what they want to hear?

Politicians must hide the truth in order to do their jobs. Jean-Claude Junker, the Prime Minister of Luxembourg and head of the European Union at one point said, "When it becomes serious, you have to lie."

The first rule of politics: never believe anything until it's been officially denied.

Only a politician would tell you everything is well because his entire future consists of being re-elected. He is not concerned about any disasters that may happen in the long term as that is someone else's problem. It is the now that is important; therefore if he cannot fix it now, he kicks the can down the street for someone else to fix in the future. Too often the long-term consequences, or the secondary effects, of an action are well and truly ignored.

When things do go well for politicians, by pure chance, they pretend it was due to them and their plans but their only skill is pretending that is how they wanted it to turn out from the start.

The politicians in a democratic society are usually slow, short-sighted, and soft-handed while the politicians in a social society tries to think for the citizens as they assume they are all incapable.

Politicians want more power and they know that crises and panics are the best opportunities to get people to surrender their freedom for the promise of security.

Since the Renaissance, banking and governance have gone hand in hand. In greasing the wheels of economic development, and funding ventures, financiers have made and broken political dynasties for centuries. It is a fact of life that the most economic nations have been those with powerful banks.

Although government's relationship with finance has been almost unavoidable, the concentration of power in the hands of financial elites and the privileges they receive from political protection became a contentious issue.

The right of a government to rule over the citizens of a nation is not absolute. Therefore it is wrong to abuse them or conduct genocide against a portion of the populace.

The Universal Declaration of Human Rights was adopted in 1948 as "the foundation of freedom, justice and peace in the world." This was a bold and clear commitment that power would no longer serve as a cover to oppress or injure people, and it established qual rights of all people to life, liberty, security of person, equal protection of the law and freedom from torture, arbitrary detention or forced exile."

Therefore the world powers should intervene in countries where the citizens are abused and protect them as a moral responsibility and having a legal right to do so; but without a war which can cause even more misery upon its citizens.

The question we have to ask ourselves is; can we live with ourselves, as people, if we have the power to prevent unspeakable evil, and yet the politicians do nothing unless they can benefit from the situation. There was nothing for them in Bosnia, Rwanda, Sri Lanka, North

Korea and Zimbabwe and they did not respond to the plight of the people in need.

The politicians stimulate the economy by printing excess money which will get them votes, but they are not concerned about the hyperinflation they will cause in the future.

Examples of politicians' behaviour;

a) In 1933, Franklin D, Roosevelt took the dollar off the gold standard as Great Britain, Japan and the Scandinavia had left the gold standard in 1931, prompting foreigners to turn to the U.S. for gold. The run on the nation's gold dangerously shrank the money supply. To halt the gold run Roosevelt pronounced the country officially bankrupt and declared a national emergency.

On March 3, 1933 he closed the banks and they had to turn in all their gold to the Treasury at Fort Knox to stop the gold run.

He changed the Federal Reserve Note from a promise to pay in gold into legal tender itself backed by "the full faith and credit of the United States." All gold coins, gold bullion, and gold certificates held by public were ordered to be handed over to the U.S. Treasury, under threat of a $10,000 fine and a ten year imprisonment.

Private gold owners were paid $20.67 per ounce and then the price of gold was raised to $35 per ounce, reducing the value of the dollar. The Federal Reserve also had to turn in its gold but the Fed was paid in gold certificates (paper money redeemable in gold).

Roosevelt was accused of dishonesty to protect the currency to pay the gambling debts of the International Bankers. Roosevelt then implemented the Glass-Steagall Act against the Wall Street looting and corruption that had brought down the stock market and the economy. Regular commercial banks were separated from investment banks dealing with stocks and bonds.

b) In 1971, President Richard Nixon, without the approval of Congress, permanently took the dollar off the gold standard and changed the rules of money-not just for the United States, but also for the world. This change was one in a series of changes leading to our current financial crisis that began in 2007.

When Nixon changed the rules of money with gold being separate from the dollar the Western world entered a period of extreme financial instability. Inflation went through the roof while the rich got richer.

Things You Should Know

c) The Reagan administration, as well as the Bush administration that followed it implemented a monumental programme of military spending and tax reduction for the rich to curb the tight credit programs. This kept the economy ticking over at the expense of running unprecedented deficits.

d) President George Bush Sr. openly approved the bailouts of various companies especially the Long Term Capital Management engineered during his term of office. He used taxes to bail out banks with $66 billion that were experiencing difficulties meeting their commitments. He said, 'This legislation will safeguard and stabilise America's financial system and put in place permanent reforms so these problems will never happen again'. The rescue package eventually cost taxpayers over $150 billion.

The public cost was very obvious to the taxpayers and the more solvent of the banks, which paid higher insurance premiums. Bush senior's actions prevented him from winning a second term in office.

e) In 1999 Congress and President Bill Clinton repealed the Glass-Steagall Act of 1933, which had, for sixty six years maintained barriers between lending banks and securities houses. The repealing was done to legitimize the formation of Citigroup, the biggest "financial supermarket" in U.S. history.

Although there had been a small but growing market in credit-based derivative products in the 1990's, the rule changes of 1999 laid the groundwork for massive growth in that market. It turned into a massive increase in leverage. The sale of questionable products to un-expectant buyers was supported by bankrupt companies.

Bill Clinton and his wife were implicated in the failure of Madison Guaranty Savings and Loan.

f) In 2004 George W Bush created $3 trillion in tax cuts when the budget was in deficit. All he did was borrowed more money which one day would have to be repaid with interest, which is absolute madness. The tax cuts were supposed to be temporary but the Bush administration created them knowing that future legislatures would find it almost intolerably hard not to extend them, so temporary came to mean permanent.

He distorted the reasons for going to war, refused to allow coffins being airlifted back to America from Iraq and Afghanistan to be filmed by the media and concealed the terrible effect of the war on the lives of ordinary Iraqi civilians.

He used almost the same words as his father when he bailed out the banks with $700 billion because they were elected to protect the system-not to fix it. The Bush family was directly involved with the failure of Silverado Savings and Loan.

When the economy slowed and the number of foreclosures mounted and the consumer spending dried up President Bush had maintained that there was only a little ripple in the housing market and a few homeowners would be hurt. As the housing market fell to a fourteen-year low, he reassured the nation on October 17, 2007: "I feel good about many of the economic indicators here in the United States."

On November 13, he reassuringly said, "The underpinnings of our economy are strong, and we're a resilient economy." But conditions in the banking and real estate sectors continued to worsen. As the economy went into recession in December 2007, he began to admit that there might be a problem. "There's definitely some storm clouds and concerns, but the underpinning is good."

Even when the country had been in a recession for a couple of months, he refused to admit it, declaring on February 2008, "I don't think we're headed to a recession.

After a loss of some 1.8 million jobs and a decrease of 24 percent in the Dow Jones average, President Bush and his advisers insisted that things were not as bad as they appeared.

g) Faced with a projection that the costs of Medicare and Medicaid were spiralling out of control the Obama administration rolled out the Obama-care without any cost control. The Obama-care programme was to be used to increase the scope of health care across America and it would help to reduce the budget deficit by $119 billion over ten years, this without even calculating the costs. The reform would increase costs and causes an additional burden of insane proportions upon the U.S. populace.

21. Government Statistics

With modern technology analysts are able to handle masses of data in a fraction of the time it used to take. This data must still be interpreted, which requires the knowledge to comprehend the data, the knowledge to use the data and the ability to understand the restrictions of said data. Even with the spectacular amount of data available these days it does not necessarily go along with increased accuracy.

Things You Should Know

Even a fairly simple concept such as population is ambiguous: does it refer to *de jure* population or to the *de facto* population? What you also have to consider is that a considerable amount of data has not been collected by data agencies but are a by-product of the one or other administration process. Someone once said, 'if you torture the data long enough, they will confess.'

It should be quite simple to measure inflation. If you buy a basket of goods in the beginning of the financial year for $100, and you buy the same items at the end of the financial year for $109 the calculated inflation would be 9% for the year.

This however is not the way most governments care to measure it. They prefer to calculate it taking substitution, hedonic quality modelling, geometric weighting and home owner's equivalent rent into consideration.

Substitution; Let's suppose that in the beginning your selected basket of goods contained a litre of milk, priced at $2.00 but at the end of the year the price of that milk had gone up to $2.80, (40% increase). Because you aren't a passive consumer, obliged to buy the same items you bought in the beginning you're likely to reject the milk as being unacceptably expensive and buy something else. Consumers are naturally astute shoppers and they stock up on the good deals available at the time.

André Klopper

Hedonic quality modelling lowers reported prices to account for changes deemed to be quality improvements. If new cars have airbags and new computers are faster, statisticians shave a bit from their actual prices to reflect the perception that they offer more for the money than previous versions.

Geometric weighting happens when rising components are given less relative weight.

Homeowners' equivalent rent replaces what it actually costs to buy a house with an estimate of what homeowners would have to pay to rent their homes- adjusted hedonically for quality improvements. When the home prices are rising faster than the rents as they have been for the past couple of decades, the change lowers the impact of housing on inflation.

There is no absolute and objective gauge of inflation and any particular measure is simply one way of making up the calculation, based on a host of assumptions.

The problem for statisticians is how to handle this consumer behaviour. Government statisticians prefer to avoid the clarity and rigor of the old method, to re-weigh the basket in a way that reflects consumer efforts to avoid price increases and to generate an inflation rate far lower than the one we actually experience.

Some governments replace the Consumer

Price Index (CPI) with Personal Consumer Expenditure (PCE) that excludes food and energy prices.

There are four reasons governments want to publish low inflation rates:

1. It shows they are in control
2. Lower payments to the people on pensions and social security.
3. Managing people's expectations
4. Protect its currency

Needless to say, there is no question that consumers don't feel like they're in a low-inflation environment when they go to the supermarket or the petrol station and experience rising prices.

Gross Domestic Product (GDP) is the basic measure of national income, the total value of goods and services produced in a given period of time. Nearly always GDP is quoted as an aggregate figure; offering us a measure of the value created by an entire economy over a given quarter or year. Underpinning that aggregate figure is a massive amount of detailed data about every sector and sub-sector of the country's economy. The data are churned out with an impressive degree of timelines, by the government statisticians who publish large quantities of reports and make data available online.

The data however are recalculated in the same manner as the inflation data. It is not the real GDP that gets published but the adjusted GDP which the politicians have accepted.

Other statistics sometimes also need a good massage such as unemployment. America reported almost acceptable unemployment level of 7% in 2013. This measure however left out a few critical things; people losing their high-paying jobs and only being able to find part-time minimum wage jobs are not included. People who are so discouraged after losing their jobs and unable to find work that they just stop looking for work, are not counted as unemployed because they have "left the workforce."

The *New York Post* reported that Census Bureau analysts allegedly under orders from superiors, fabricated data that went into unemployment reports leading up to the 2012 presidential election.

22. The Ponzi Schemes

At the end of World War 1 inflation, debt, and flu were causing havoc in the world. The prices of the International Reply Coupons (IRC) had become seriously misaligned and Charles

Ponzi realized he could make profit from it.

He quit his job and borrowed money and wired it to his relatives in Italy to buy IRC and send them to him. He tried to sell the IRC's in Boston but red tape and bureaucracy thwarted his efforts. Determined, he explained to his friends in Boston about his vast wealth, IRC scheme and promised to double their money in ninety days. Some people thought the offer sounded too good to be true and kept their money to themselves. Others couldn't resist and handed over their cash and Ponzi was in business.

Within five months Ponzi made $400,000 and if investors wanted their money back they were paid. The retiring investors were paid out by the money paid in by new investors. The old investors told everyone they knew how they made huge profits and the money continued to pour in. Ponzi deposited $3 million in a Boston bank then bought a controlling interest in it. He lived in luxury, owned a mansion with air conditioning and a swimming pool.

Ponzi received all the incoming money and placed some of it in the bank at 5% interest and the rest he just spent as if there were no tomorrow. Offering 50% returns every forty five days his liabilities expanded by 50% in the same period while his assets were shrinking as he raided it.

The whole house of cards collapsed and many people lost their life savings some even lost their homes. Within a year of beginning his scheme Ponzi surrendered to the federal authorities and was sentenced to five years in prison. When he was released he was immediately re-indicted and was sentenced for another seven years in prison. After his release he died unknown in poverty in a charitable hospital in Rio de Janeiro.

Schemes in which depositors can only be paid out by using the money of new investors are called Ponzi schemes. As long as the scheme is expanding, everything looks fine. As the investors became wiser with time, so have Ponzi schemes become shrewder.

Bernie Madoff, former chairman of the board of the National Association of Securities Dealers, former member of the Securities Industry Association, and former chairman of NASDAQ operated a Ponzi scheme under the guise of a hedge fund.

When his scheme hit the wall in 2008, investors had accumulated losses of $18 billion. Madoff was sentenced to jail for a term of 150 years, the maximum allowed.

The world's third biggest Ponzi scheme was run by Adriaan Niewoudt, the man behind the notorious rotten milk Ponzi scheme that took South Africa by storm in the early 1980s when he launched his money-making venture.

After his grandmother showed him a milk culture she used as a skin product he turned the culture into a work-from-home business by selling dried plants that would produce thick milk for R500, which would produce 10 jars of culture a week.

In return he paid R10 per envelope or R100 per week for producers who sent him a teaspoon of the culture, making it possible to break even within five weeks. The dried product sent back by activation kit buyers were ground up without first being removed from the envelopes in which it was shipped, and resold as new activators.

Niewoudt raised a reported R140 million through his 'milk culture' project and thousands of South Africans fell for it, furiously buying the mixture of cheese and milk culture from Niewoudt, growing it in glasses and then drying it into a powder to re-sell to Niewoudt and recruiting others to do the same, a classic pyramid scheme.

At the time Niewoudt claimed that he needed vast quantities of the dried powder to develop a skin cream product. There never was such a product and investigators found the milk culture was simply a cover for a Ponzi scheme.

Tons of dried milk-culture was found rotting in his shed.

The Ponzi scheme finally collapsed and Niewoudt's assets were sequestrated. He was found guilty of diamond theft and illegal diamond dealing in the 1990s and sentenced to eight years in jail.

According to subsequent evidence presented at trial, the Kubus business was exported to the United States in 1984. By late 1984 several corporations had been established around the product. They sold 'activator kits' that allowed the making of the milk culture for $350 per a minimum of ten kits. These cultures were utilised in manufacturing cosmetics.

Niewoudt served only a year before being released. Since the collapse of the Kubus scheme, he has been involved in several controversial money-making schemes.

Ponzi schemes are easy to spot as they're so dumb, and so obvious, but people don't spot them because they don't like to face uncomfortable truths or they trust people too much. Some people confuse Ponzi schemes with pyramid schemes. This is inaccurate. The essence of a Ponzi scheme is deception. The investor thinks that the promised high return on their investment will come from the promoter's putting the investment to work, not that their investment will be used to pay other investors in order to keep the scheme going.

There need be no deception in a pyramid scheme where a person pays a fee to become a retail seller of a product and is promised a fee of any other retail seller whom they recruit. Eventually there are no more recruits, and that is what happens in a speculative bubble which must eventually stop expanding and then burst. A pyramid scheme is a form of gambling.

23. Derivatives

A derivative as the name implies is nothing more than a contract whose value derives from some other asset, a bond, a stock, a quantity of gold. Key to derivatives is that those who buy and sell them are each making a bet on the future value of that asset.

Versions of derivative trading have existed for centuries. Rudimentary examples of futures and options contracts have been found on clay tablets from Mesopotamia dating from 1750 BC. In the twelfth and thirteenth centuries English monasteries made futures deals with foreign merchants to sell wool up to twenty years in advance. During the seventeenth-century Holland when the tulip prices began to soar, merchants' frantic buying and selling of tulip futures led to a craze that ended in a spectacular crash.

It is difficult to pinpoint the exact origin of the concept of credit derivatives. Since the 1980's American banks began trading credit derivatives. By the early 1990's the wider investing world had absolutely no idea how credit derivatives were producing such phenomenal growth. Those who had inside knowledge tended to revel in its air of mystery.

The derivatives teams worked on ways to push money around the world in a more efficient manner and they used computing power and high order mathematics to achieve this. They used their 'innovations' in bold new ways to generate returns.

After the world's first currency swap was concluded between IBM and the World Bank worth $210 million for ten years; the new form of trade spread fast across Wall Street and the City of London. The swap mutated into complex deals giving bankers almost unlimited power.

With the new derivatives bankers could dismember existing assets or contracts and write contracts that resurrected them in entirely new ways, earning huge fees. The young traders were thrilled with the increasing power, and freedom they enjoyed. Few at the banks outside the derivatives team itself knew how the team worked as they would only reveal the scantiest details about their business.

From time to time senior management would try to clip the derivatives teams' wings but they were given great autonomy and had to back down. As the derivatives market grew the traders basked in the knowledge that they were producing an escalating share of the bank's profits, The derivatives traders were united with their fascination with deconstructing financial instruments and their belief in the efficiency, and superiority of free markets.

They asserted that market prices were always right and the only true guide to what anything should be worth. Market discipline is the best form of discipline as markets can correct excess far better than any government.

The rush into derivatives was partly driven by aggressive marketing efforts by the banks and regulatory changes in the asset management world. Another factor that fuelled the trend was falling interest rates. Falling rates made it harder for investment managers to earn decent returns by purchasing relatively risk-free government or corporate bonds, therefore bond investors looked at the derivative market.

The herd instinct was amazing as every investor was looking at yield and the derivatives traders created new products with higher risks and returns. When Greenspan suddenly raised the interest rates in 1994 it stunned the markets, triggering a sharp fall in bond prices. The derivatives deals during the previous two years were based on rates continuing to fall and with the sudden hike these deals produced enormous losses.

The losses prompted investor and public fury and the media unleashed a torrent of criticism. America's General Accounting Office issued a highly critical 196-page study on the state of the derivatives world. They declared there was significant gaps and weaknesses in risk management so dangerous that Congress needed to step in.

Congress swiftly responded and four bills proposing regulations were submitted, but the Wall Street lobbying campaign was so effective that all four of the anti-derivatives bills in Congress were shelved. Self-policing had won the day, and that was to make all the difference.

A new product Credit Default Swap (CDS) was developed to reduce the imposed absolute limits on the amount of money that could be loaned to given sectors. It overturned one of the fundamental rules of banking that default risk is an inevitable liability of the business. CDS made it possible for banks to make loans without carrying all, or perhaps even any of the risk involved.

With credit derivatives banks could fine tune risk burdens, releasing banks from constraints and freeing up vast amounts of capital, turbo charging not only banking but the whole economy.

When the Fed issued a statement in 1996 suggesting that banks would be allowed to reduce capital reserves by using credit derivatives the traders began selling the idea to their colleagues. It was a hard sell to the more traditional bankers who had spent their careers evaluating loan risks and they reacted with horror.

For months the two opposing forces battled it out until the Asia crisis broke the deadlock. The commercial banks suffered losses and they took decisive actions to improve their profits. The bankers came up with the idea of bundling up large quantities of loan packages that would spread the risk of any problematic loans over the whole bundle. They also realised they could use the cash flow from the mortgage payments made on that bundle of loans to make a tidy profit and the business boomed.

To complete the scheme they created shell companies specifically for buying bundles of mortgages and selling the securities made from them. These companies were usually located in offshore jurisdictions to ensure they did not incur U.S. tax.

The traders were jubilant when the credit derivatives took off and they thought they were the smartest people on the planet when they found a way to by-pass the Basel rules. The reserves were relaxed on the Reserve Bank dropping the reserves to be held on every $10 billion from $800 million to just $160 million.

When they started to trade with mortgages the data showed the housing market had never been in a price slump since the Great Depression. Goldman Sachs masking the true value of investments, then selling those worthless investments to customers while placing bets on those same investments would eventually fail. The most notorious example was the Timberwolf deal which brought down an Australian hedge fund, and which Goldman Sachs bankers e-mailed to each other bragging, "Boy that Timberwolf was one shitty deal."

24. The Banking Crises

Market crises are almost as old as the invention of money but the following banking crises were not triggered by wars. The relevant question here is why did bankers, regulators and investors invested in a system that was doomed to self-destruct? Did they fail to see the flaws, or did they fail to care?

Greece

For most of the 1980's and 1990's, Greek interest rates had run a full 10 percent higher than the German ones. The huge difference in rates tell us that investors knew perfectly well the Greek government could not be trusted to repay its loans without destroying value. There was no consumer credit in Greece; Greeks didn't have credit cards.

Greece had a history of falsifying its national accounts; their deficits were high, corruption rife, there was huge tax avoidance and a dysfunctional government. They wished to be treated like a properly functioning Northern European country by dropping their currency and adopting the euro.

In 2001, Goldman Sachs secretly helped Greece hide billions of dollars of debt through the use of complex financial instruments such as credit default swaps. Greece fulfilled the national targets by a flurry of statistical manipulation and with the aid of Goldman Sachs they obtained the targets and were accepted.

Greece entered the European Monetary Union, swapped the drachma for the euro, some observers however noted that the Greek numbers never seemed to add up. Once accepted Greece was allowed to spend lavishly on extensive welfare while racking up untenable fiscal deficits.

When Greece entered the Euro-zone default was left as the only plausible option. To remain in the euro zone they had to maintain budget deficits below 3 percent of GDP. They falsified their accounting records again to show they were hitting the targets.

Always looking ahead Goldman Sachs protected itself from the Greek debt bubble by betting against Greek bonds, obviously expecting that they would eventually fail.

When the tsunami of cheap credit rolled across the planet between 2002 and 2007 the corruption was high in the Greek public service. The money was stolen or squandered by the officials in the Greek government. The cheap credit wasn't just money it was temptation which pushed the country into moral collapse.

Most of the eleven million Greeks believed it was their right not to pay taxes. The Greek courts took up to fifteen years to resolve tax cases. Only the salaried workers paid their full taxes as their taxes were withheld from their pay checks. To avoid paying taxes Greeks were self-employed, making them the highest percentage self-employed workers in Europe.

It was assumed that anyone who was working for the Greek government is meant to be bribed. The total absence of faith in one another is self-reinforcing and the epidemic of lying, cheating and stealing makes any sort of civic life impossible; the collapse of civic life only encourages more lying, cheating and stealing.

With the credit crisis of 2007/8, every single one of the major rating agencies rated Greece at least A-, or upper medium grade. Impossible but true. In 2009, the sudden revelation of the dire state of the government's finances soon sparked a funding crisis.

The banks didn't sink the country, the country sank the banks. Greece's money was borrowed by the state; the debts are the debts of the Greek people but the people want no part of them. They still refused to pay their taxes and blamed everybody for their financial ruin but themselves. They accumulated $1.2 trillion in debts.

Greek Prime minister Papandreou wanted to leave it up to the citizens to decide whether or not staying in the Euro-zone in exchange for harsh austerity measures was in their national best interest.

Global bankers panicked and in less than a

week fearing the Greek people would vote to withdraw from the Euro-zone the bankers at the European Central Bank and the IMF took away democracy in Greece. They forced Papandreou to scrap the idea of a national referendum and replaced him with former vice president of the European Central Bank, Lucas Papademos.

The government announced several packages of austerity measures to close the gap but the markets were unconvinced by the Greek plans and the cost of Greek borrowing rose alarmingly. The workers responded with strikes and violent protest.

Trade stopped with Greece which disrupted supplies causing shortages of inputs which in turn began halting the manufacturing processes. Greece found itself in the throes of financial, commercial and political collapse. There were runs on banks as the people tried to cash out and expatriated their savings; pharmacies run out of medicine and many other imports ran short; nationally elected officials were replaced with political appointees whose candidacies were vetted by the countries creditors.

In July the Greek government bowed down to outside pressure and started selling their islands, golf courses, beaches, airports and their farmlands to repay their debt.

Greece had reached the stage where debt is not acceptable to global investors, and it had to piggyback on the creditworthiness of its neighbours. Investors simply do not believe that the Greek government, on its own, can repay its creditors in full.

As long as Greece has the euro they do not have the option to reduce their debt by hyperinflation or deflation. They are stuck, if they leave the euro they might be more competitive with very low exchange rates but by leaving the euro might annoy other European countries and deprive Greece of their support.

Any hint of euro departure would cause Greek depositors to withdraw their money and deposit it in Europe, the result would be a run on the banks.

Ireland

From the late 1980's Ireland emerged from a lengthy period of economic stagnation marked by high unemployment, emigration and crippling public debt despite high tax levels. The government tackled the debt problem with tough spending restraint and managed to negotiate a series of social partnership agreements. This caused wage rate moderation and industrial peace in return for income tax concessions. The EU structural funds were used to fund an expanded infrastructural program.

These policies and the growth in export caused real GDP to expand 6% per annum, unemployment to drop from 16% to 5%, poverty fell from 15% of the population to 5% of the population making Ireland the frontier of economic prosperity. It was called the "Celtic Tiger" boom which started in the late 1980's and brought sustained growth in employment and income. As Ireland became a founder member of the euro-zone, they experienced a dramatic drop in interest rates.

For centuries, the Irish had dreamed of being like the Americans and now their dreams have come true. For the population of 4.5 million it was a tale of misery, struggle, transformation and triumph. The small country showed the world that with a radical course of slashing expenditures and reducing tax rates, and regulations they can soar.

In 1986 the Irish GDP per head was 66% of EU average, in 1991 it was 75% and in 1999 it was 111% of the EU average. The Irish people felt a lot better about themselves. Ireland had become prosperous because its workers were unusually productive and it was exporting goods that people wanted to buy.

Unlike the Icelanders who invested most of their money in assets abroad during their banking boom, the Celtic people invested in themselves and their own homes. The Irish obsession with having a secure home was rooted in a history of eviction and displacement. This was depicted by the fact that 87% of Irish households own their own homes, compared to an EU average of 61%.

The sharp fall in nominal and real interest triggered the housing price surge. This led to a sharp increase in construction and housing well beyond population needs. Between 1996 and 2006 there were 347,000 new households formed in Ireland and over the same period 597,000 new houses were built. This caused an oversupply of 30% in Leitrim and 12% in Dublin. The houses were built on the hope of a quick profit but some might never be occupied. While the houses were being built, Irish labourers had jobs and the result was rapid GDP growth.

The three-fold increase in average real property prices from 1994 to 2006 was the highest in any advanced economy as property prices developed their own momentum and overshot equilibrium levels. Ireland was placed at the head of the wealthiest nations of Europe. Between 1994 and 2006, the average second-hand house price in Dublin increased from €82,772 to €512,461 a rise of 5.2 times.

Economists stated long before the housing

bust that the housing prices seemed unsustainable, and hoped for a soft landing without a significant rise in unemployment.

For the first four years of the boom the banks did not appear to have played a leading role but from 2003 the housing bubble was clearly bank driven. The banks competed aggressively with stimulating demand innovations such as 100% LTV mortgages, this result in declining credit requirements. In the long term, it was a disastrous strategy, leaving the country with houses no one wanted and debts that cannot be repaid.

The housing boom fuelled a massive growth in private sector credit. In 2004 private credit stood at €190 billion, in 2006 it was €305 billion and by 2008 hit €400 billion, two and a half times the GDP. This created an obvious instability in the Irish economy.

The Irish banks were fatally weakened by a deep involvement in the property bubble which swelled based on huge capital inflows, this sustained by a belief that equilibrium house prices would soar and that housing demand would continue to grow for the foreseeable future.

Ireland experienced a steady growth in their exports until it peaked in 2002 and then began to decline every year after. The shortfall in the balance of payment was filled by enormous levels of borrowing. Consumption replaced production and building replaced manufacturing.

Without any proper calculations the finance minister, Charlie MacCreevy announced free GP services to all those over seventy. He calculated that to cover the 39,000 people it would cost €19 million. In fact the very first year it covered 63,000 people at a cost of €126 million.

From the mid-1990 onwards, it became ever more undeniable that corruption was deeply embedded, both at the top and the bottom of Irish public life. It became completely clear that the public interest was being literally sold out to an inner circle of businessmen.

The Irish banks had been colluding, on a massive scale with fraud, tax evasion and routine breaches of exchange control laws. Large sections of the Irish business class, from strong farmers to the chairmen of blue chip companies were hiding money in offshore accounts, or claiming to be living outside the country when they were making money within the Irish borders.

The state authorities knew about the widespread organised crime committed by financial institutions and their customers and did nothing to stop it.

The financial crisis of 2007/8 caused two problems for Irish banks. Firstly, with no new money to borrow, withdrawal of deposits caused a liquidity problem. The second problem was solvency which was far more serious. With the value of their assets declining in line with the property market the liabilities of the banks were now considerably greater than their assets. Insolvency loomed as the major Irish banks approached the government for assistance.

There was a broad consensus in the government that nationalising the Anglo Irish Bank and government interventions to stabilise the other banks was in the best interest of the country. The government also introduced an extensive guarantee of deposits and other liabilities and had to write off €25 billion in unrecoverable capital injections into Anglo Irish Bank and INBS.

The European Commission in Brussels publicly rebuked the Irish government for failing to control the public finances during the boom years. The International Monetary Fund was predicting that Ireland's GDP would shrink by 13.5% in 2009 and 2010, the worst performance among all the advanced economies.

The economic consequences of the crash have been severe. The recession in Ireland was driven by a dramatic decline in construction investment and a decline in domestic consumption. Banks pulled in lending which amplified the downturn in the property sector. The increase in bad loans further curtailed the supply of credit by Irish banks. The recession has led to a sharp increase in unemployment to 14%.

House prices dropped between 30 and 50 percent and it was pretty traumatic for people who had bought homes during the boom years.

Ireland reduced its debt by borrowing from the ECB to bail out their banks. The loans were then transformed into 40-year bonds with the help of very clever inventive legal-council.

Iceland

The country Iceland was formed by the tribal democracy of the Norse between 874 and 930 AD when they founded the Alpingi. The harsh climate with its cold sunlight-deprived winters and isolated location, limits the number of people willing to live there.

Iceland has a population of three hundred thousand hardy people and small enough to make direct democracy work, a nation so tiny and homogeneous that everyone in it knows pretty much everyone else. Beyond a certain size it becomes impossible to get anything done without acting through representatives. One of the benefits of life inside such a small nation is that nothing needs to be explained; everyone already knows everything that needs to be known.

The ancient society based its economy on the North Sea fishery until they diversified into energy and aluminium production. During the 1980's David Oddsson, the prime minister, went on a quest to give Icelandic people their freedom from government control. He lowered taxes, privatized industry, freed up trade and in 2002 privatized the banks.

The government had enacted legislation in 1999 concerning international trading companies which set tax rates and regulations for foreign companies registering in Iceland. According to this law, the revenues of foreign companies registering in Iceland were taxed at a very low rate of 5 percent, this making Iceland competitive with offshore tax havens. These companies were also freed from having to pay property taxes or customs duties, all for a very reasonable registration fee of $1,400 a year. This set up Iceland as an offshore tax haven and business centre.

Foreign companies registering in Iceland received the status of normal Icelandic international businesses, Iceland's status as a European nation and a member of NATO allowed them to escape the scrutiny of central banks.

The depositors from the U.K. and Netherlands foolishly thought that there was a "free Lunch"; they could get higher returns without risk. Perhaps they also foolishly thought though their own governments were doing their regulatory job. But, as everywhere, regulators had largely assumed that markets would take care of themselves.

What the Icelandic bankers took to heart from their American counterparts was to buy as many assets as possible with borrowed money, as assets prices only rose. By 2007, Icelanders owned roughly fifty times more foreign assets than they had in 2002. As the financial system grew to many times its capital base, Iceland began to resemble a hedge fund.

In 2003, Iceland's three biggest banks had assets of only a few billion dollars, about 100 percent of the country's gross domestic product. Over the next three and a half years the banking assets grew to over $140 billion and their combined worth was more than eleven times the country's GDP.

People gave up traditional jobs in the fishing industry and farming to work in banks or got into property speculation. They obtained cheap loans with bank officers often convincing them to double the size of their requests, whilst assuring them of affordable interest rates on their debts.

The value of Icelandic stocks and real estate went through the roof. With the collapse of Lehman Brothers in the U.S. Kaupthing's finances soured. From 2003 to 2007 while the value of the U.S. stock market was doubling, the value of the Icelandic stock market multiplied nine times, while the exchange rate of the local currency the krona increased sharply.

The brash young bankers took the UK, Scandinavian and mainland European banking markets by storm, conquering the sophisticated investment banking markets.

The Icelandic people were warned by outsiders that they had a problem and were heading for a disaster; but they were greeted with anger and the Iceland bankers threatened them with lawsuits.

In September of 2008 the Icelandic economy was in dire straits as the country was brought to the brink of bankruptcy. There was a 90 percent plunge in the stock market, 60 percent of which consisted of shares in the three banks that were going bankrupt.

Gordon Brown, Prime Minister of Britain made a decision to invoke anti-terrorism legislation against Iceland in order to freeze the assets of Kaupthing, Iceland's biggest bank, forcing it to suspend operations.

The Icelandic Central Bank spent $280 million of its reserves trying to support the banks whilst jacking up the interest rates to 12 percent to entice money back to the country as hedge funds dumped the krona. It proved futile as the foreign debts dwarfed the central bank's resources.

There was a ninefold rise in unemployment. Inflation shot up to 18 percent, with the Icelandic currency falling 50 percent against the U.S. dollar.

Iceland effectively went bust their 300,000 citizens found that they bore the responsibility for $100 billion in banking losses. Their debts amounted to 8.5 times their GDP. The Icelanders suffered, as most of them were hungry but too ashamed to ask for handouts.

Geir Haarde, Iceland's prime minister dismissed the government when the public outcry forced him to resign. Much of the political battle focussed on whether it was fair for Iceland's tiny population to be held financially responsible for the overseas losses incurred by the country's privately owned banks.

Grimsson the new Prime minister held a national referendum. The Icelanders were angered by how they were exploited and stood up against the powerful financial forces when the majority of them voted against paying the bank's debt.

The British and Dutch argued that a private bank could operate anywhere in Europe, and when it succeeded the bankers got extraordinary benefits and the shareholders obtained huge profits. But when it failed, the bill had to be paid by the citizens.

With the referendum the Icelanders sent a signal to the bankers that they can be irresponsible and daring, and if they are lucky become very rich, but if they fail, other people will not pay for their mistakes. Every government in Europe was very upset with this move but the Icelanders had voted against the bailing out of the banks.

With drastic reforms and a sharp devaluation of the krona the Icelanders found a base of stability upon which they fixed their economy. They reduced their once global banks to a size more befitting their small island economy. The local krona currency collapsed under the pressure. A few months later the country adapted the euro and the krona ceased to exist.

25. Cycles And Trends

Cycle: a series of events or operations that are regularly repeated in the same order eg, the boom and bust periods of the economic cycle. Economic cycles involve expansion, pause and contraction, and could be short term or long term. The economic cycle is neutral just like the weather or the ocean tide; it's neither good nor bad.

We have adapted to the weather's seasonal changes and dress accordingly to the weather and participate in sports suitable for that season eg, skiing in the winter and swimming in the summer.

Just as we dress differently in winter and summer, so must we modify our behaviour to suit the current stage of the economic cycle. A behaviour that was successful in one part of the cycle can fail miserably or be disastrous in another part of the cycle.

Although economic, market, and property cycles are in a repetitive pattern they are not completely predictable. They are not like a set of traffic lights-perfectly synchronised, orderly and with clear indications for all sides to see. There's an old stock market saying, 'No one rings a bell at the top or bottom of the market.'

History and experience showed us that a period of growth is usually followed by an adjustment, and sometimes by a time of stagnant or negative growth. Markets can crash, or they can soften gradually or stagnate. A general rule is that the larger the rise, the sharper the fall that follows.

From a historical perspective, what is happening today is depressingly familiar. Over the centuries hundreds of societies have borrowed too much and then destroyed the currency in which their debts were denominated. All these cycles begin with the assumption that we are emotional creatures with limited, selective memories, condemned to repeat the past because we don't remember it.

Business people spend time analysing patterns and cycles to understand the implications and consequences of these patterns. They analyse the duration, the stability, the range and speed of change and the indicators, drivers and influences. Their goal is to forecast future changes with some accuracy, to plan and adapt their behaviour to those changes. By predicting the phases of the cycles, not only are they protecting their wealth but can gain financially.

Is timing is everything?

Things You Should Know

The single most sought-after advice must be timing. One of the most important decision regarding financial matters is timing, whether buying a house, a car, insurance, or an investment. Buyer's remorse quickly set in if they recalculate how different their purchase might have been if bought yesterday or a month later.

Experience has taught us however, that over the short term it's almost impossible to do much better than chance.

Some people are so obsessed with the correct timing of their investment that they fail to invest. Their fear of wrong timing lead to inactivity and they therefore lose out on golden opportunities.

Specialists routinely imply that they have some methodology that will help you get the timing right to invest. Most people are impressed by a visual presentation showing trends in the market as they are led to believe that all the information they need is reflected in the past history of the matter in hand.

However, many specialists believe that the short period on which their assumptions are based will continue indefinite. They are unwilling to accept that cycles are a fact of life and their equations fail to take it in to consideration.

The economic cycle is an economic phenomenon that recognises the cyclical pattern of good times following bad and that as investor you must operate against the trend by acquiring assets when the cycle is in a downward pattern.

Governments have learned through experience that the way to deal with an economic slowdown is to stimulate growth with a fast infusion of cash. They can do it by lowering interest rates, increasing spending, or lowering taxes.

Correspondingly, when the economy grows too quickly causing inflation, the government will respond by raising interest rates, raising taxes, and decreasing government spending.

Bubble: a thin ball of liquid encompassing air or gas.

In financial terms it means the market growing to such proportions and fuelled by debt that it becomes very fragile, too large and no longer sustainable, an illusory inflation in price that is grossly out of proportion to underlying values.

In his book, *The bubble of American*

Supremacy, financier George Soros explains how a market 'bubble' comes about: The process begins when a prevailing trend and a prevailing bias reinforce each other. The bias becomes more pronounced, it becomes vulnerable to being corrected by the evidence. As long as the trend survives the test it serves to reinforce the bias so that the bias can become quite far removed from reality. Eventually there arrives a moment of truth when participants become aware of the gap that separates their views from reality. A twilight period when the trend is no longer reinforced by the belief ensues. In due course the trend is also reversed and a self-correcting process is set in motion in the opposite direction. Depending on how far along a boom-bust process has been carried the reversal can be quite catastrophic, similar to a bubble's bursting.'

Warren Buffet said, 'It is like most trends: At the beginning, it's driven by fundamentals, then speculation takes over. As the old saying goes, what the wise man does in the beginning, fools do in the end. With any asset class that has a big move, first the fundamentals attract speculation, then the speculation becomes dominant. Once a price history develops, and people hear their neighbour made a lot of money on something, when impulse takes over.'

There is a group of people that see the future economic meltdown combined with other crises that will result in violent unrest across the world. The fact is the status quo is not an option as things will change for the worse.

The Fed lowered interest rates for equity prices to rise whilst raising the paper wealth of the U.S. households and corporations for them to borrow more, consume more, and invest more. The exploding imports drove the world economy, brought U.S. trade deficits to record levels causing massive growth of U.S. liabilities to overseas investors.

The bankers and traders got greedy and sold toxic house loans to investors and then some more inventive toxic derivatives. Things got out of hand and the Fed had to print excess money to keep their economy growing. The day of reckoning however is near when we will hit a severe recession when the Fed decides between hyperinflation and a severe correction.

Demographics

The demographic cycle has a duration of about eighty years. New technologies and generational boom and bust cycles create a sustain boom that starts in the spring, hits speed bumps in the summer with high inflation and falling generation spending that then descends into autumn bubble boom with rising generational spending and productivity, falling inflation and interest rates.

The final boom creates bubbles in financial assets and new technologies and business models that, unlike after the fallow season of winter, will pay off many decades to follow.

This is a natural cycle of boom and bust, inflation and deflation, innovation and creative destruction that is the invisible hand of the free market system that has driven us to unprecedented wealth and incomes, especially in the last century.

One major wealthy country after the next is sliding inexorably over the edge of the Demographic Cliff, which explains the increasingly volatile economic world we live in.

Real Estate

People see real estate as permanent as it does not need to be replaced like cars, furniture or food. In real estate just remodelling is mostly required now and then. People love real estate for most of them it is their single biggest asset and they believe unlike stocks which tend to move together globally their real estate is very local and regional. Hence people assume that although real estate is bursting in some areas it will not affect them.

Households in developed countries could

borrow massive amounts of money for mortgages for the first time in history. Interest rates were falling making housing more and more affordable. The countries experienced massive expansions in loan-to-income ratios due to huge Baby Boom demand, falling mortgage rates and limited supply in the cities.

We have seen the greatest real estate bubble in modern history, one fuelled by very low interest rates, unprecedented liberal lending and the demand of the largest generation in history. Both these trends are over or nearly over. Real estate along with infrastructure will be the sector most affected by the declining birth rates in the developed world.

The first real estate surge is in apartment rentals at around ages twenty-six to twenty-seven, when the average person gets married. The average child is born to parents, age twenty-eight. Marriage and kids create the impetus to buy a starter home which peaks around age thirty-one. But as the kids become teenagers you want a bigger home. The greatest surge in home buying comes at age thirty-seven, but it plateaus into age forty-one. Only ten percent of households buy a second home.

The second round of home buying is between ages sixty-three and sixty-five when some people move into retirement community or closer to their grandchildren. The last destination is nursing homes.

What we are experiencing now is a smaller generation following a larger one for the first time since the Black Death in Europe. The longevity of housing stock market means that, at some point, the dying of the larger, older generation will start to offset the real estate buying of the younger ones. That means increasingly supply versus demand, as the net housing demands slows and ultimately even declines when the homes of older people go back on the market and counter the need for new construction.

This is already happening in Japan and Germany where public policies are already in place for tearing down residential and commercial developments and converting them into public parks to hide the demographic decline.

The youth unemployment is very high and they simply can't afford to support a wife and kids, therefore they are much less likely to buy a house which has an impact on the real estate market.

There will be trend back towards smaller homes and more urban than suburban, especially in the coming decade. Many Baby Boomers will get stuck in larger homes that they can't sell, which will be the worst part of the real estate market until around 2024.

The question is who is going to invest in real estate when un-affordability becomes an issue and prices no longer soar but decline. The short answer is no one. Foreign buyers would flee when the economy goes sour and prices begin to crash.

Uncertainty

When people do begin to talk about problems there is always a tendency to blame someone. They want the culprit to be locked up and to suffer for what they have done, this will not solve anything but sooth our revenge.

With this news of the coming financial disaster, I certainly don't want you to panic because that does little good. Very soon however we are going to experience an economic slowdown that is going to be bigger, and will last much longer than anything we have seen before.

These are the current bubbles;

1. The real estate bubble
2. The stock market bubble
3. The private debt bubble
4. The discretionary bubble
5. The dollar bubble
6. The Western world governments' debt bubble

Rule # 1: no matter what happens, all bubbles eventually pop.

Rule # 2: no amount of optimism can change rule # 1

Life is about choices and the consequences of those choices we make.

26. Economic Recessions

Recessions and business cycles are thought to be a normal part of living in a world of inexact balances between supply and demand. Karl Marx saw recession and depression as unavoidable under a free-market capitalism as there are no restrictions on accumulations of capital other than the market itself. His viewpoint was that capitalism tends to create unbalanced accumulations of wealth, leading us to an over-accumulation of capital which inevitably leads to a crisis.

The striking thing about the seemingly endless collapse of the financial markets is how millions of ordinary people have lost huge portion of their wealth because they firmly believed the market will never fail.

André Klopper

Crisis of 1890: America

This economic depression was nearly as severe as the Great Depression of the 1930's. The bankers made loans in notes backed by gold and required repayments in notes backed by gold. The problem was there was not enough gold available to finance the needs of an expanding economy. The bankers controlled the gold, and its price was subject to manipulation by speculators.

The price of gold increased while the prices labourers obtained for their goods had dropped causing people to borrow more money. The bankers periodically contracted the money supply and the people who could not repay on such a short notice wound up losing their homes and farms to the banks.

The true wealth of the country consisted of goods and services, its resources and the creativity of its people. The farmlands were fertile and the factories ready to roll but the economy was brought to a standstill by the greedy bankers controlling the flow of the money.

To overcome the depression Congress was persuaded to borrow paper money from the bankers, and the government ended up with huge debts for money they could have printed themselves.

Crisis of 1921: Germany

Germany suspended the gold standard when it entered into World War 1 and funded the entire war by borrowing. During the war the Mark slowly declined from 4.2 to 6.7 Mark for the U.S dollar this happened at the time because of the Treaty of Versailles which had imposed crushing reparation payments on Germany. The German people were expected to reimburse the cost of the war for all participants; costs totalling three times the value of all the property in the country.

In 1921 the Mark had reached 60 Marks per U.S dollar when the 'London ultimatum' demanded reparations for war damages. After the first payment the Mark dropped to 330 Marks per U.S. dollar. Germany printed mass bank notes to buy foreign currencies to pay the reparations which worsened the inflation rates of the paper Mark.

The international reparations conferences organised by U.S. investment banker J.P Morgan Jr. failed and the inflation changed to hyperinflation causing the Mark to fall to 800 Marks per Dollar. By November 1923 the American dollar was worth 4.2 trillion German marks.

It was one of the worst runaway inflations in modern times. At its peak, a wheelbarrow full of 100 billion-mark notes could not buy a loaf of bread. People were living in hovels and starving as the total destruction of the national currency wiped out the people's savings, their businesses and the whole economy.

The important factor of the stabilisation of hyperinflation is the revaluation, and the restoration of the value of a currency depreciated by inflation. The German Government debated long and hard to be fair and balanced. The new currency, the Rentenmark, replaced the worthless Reichsbank Marks in November 1923 and twelve zeros were cut from prices, prices in the new currency remained stable.

Crisis of 1929: America

The Great Depression was a severe worldwide economic depression in the decade preceding World War II. The stock market crashed after years of accumulated private debt causing devastating effects in countries rich and poor.

The failure of Austria's biggest bank started a cascade of bank runs in Hungary, Czechoslovakia, Romania, Poland and Germany. This soon spread to all major economies. It resulted in the threat of total collapse of large financial institutions, the bailout of banks by national governments, and a period of downturns in stock markets around the world. The housing market suffered resulting in evictions, foreclosures, and prolonged unemployment.

Before the crash money was so easy to get that people were borrowing just to invest, taking out short- term, low interest loans that were readily available from the banks.

The stock market was promoted by allowing the investors to place a small payment on the stock and pay off the balance after its price went up, reaping heavy profit. This investment strategy turned the stock market into a speculative pyramid scheme, in which most of the money invested did not actually exist.

This caused a huge liquidity problem and the lack of available money forced investors to sell at a loss and the stock market crashed overnight. People withdrew their savings while foreigners withdrew their gold, further depleting the reserves. It was the biggest bank run in history and little money was available to buy goods so workers were laid off. This huge debt led to despair, a starving populace.

The American dream, the basis of capitalism was swept away with the depression when the assets of the middle class were delivered into the hands of the banks and the financial elite.

Economists were strongly influenced by Milton Friedman's argument that the Great Depression had been the result of the Federal Reserve's shrinking the money supply when prices and output fell in the wake of the stock market crash. He said that had the Fed kept up the money supply the nation would have experienced nothing worse than a recession.

The common view among economic historians is that the Great Depression ended with the advent of World War II.

John Kenneth Galbraith wrote in his book *The Great Crash 1929,* that the economy before the disaster was unsound as there was a bad distribution of income, bad banking structure and a poor state of economic intelligence. He also stated that the rich bankers had no sense of responsibility towards the community.

Crises in Russia

From September 1814 to June 1815 the Congress of Vienna was held to settle the issues of the French wars and the dissolution of the Holy Roman Empire. Behind the scenes Nathan Mayer Rothschild proposed the formation of a new world order concentrated around central banking. All the major powers, with the exception of Russia were indebted to the Rothschild banks.

Tsar Alexander I refused to comply with Rothschild or his offer to set up a central bank in Russia, instead he establish an Alliance between Austria, Prussia and Russia.

In 1860 the State Bank of the Russian Empire was founded under the direct control of the Ministry of Finance. In 1861 Tsar Alexander II abolished serfdom, which at that time affected 30% of the population. The nobility ceded land to the peasants for a very small sum. This land was held in trust by the village commune.

From 1894 the bank minted and printed the nation's coins and notes and regulated the money supply. Its vast gold reserves, the largest in the world, exceeded the bank note issue by more than 100%.

After the Stolypin Act of 1906 peasants could obtain individual title with hereditary rights and by 1913 two million families had used this opportunity to obtain their farms. Agricultural production soared during this period and Russia become the world's bread basket.

By 1914 the State Bank had become one of

the most influential lending institutions in Europe while Russia had the smallest national debt in the world. By then 80% of the arable land was in the hands of the peasants.

From 1890 to 1914 Russia's industrial production quadrupled while their increase in GDP averaged 10% per annum. Russia was the most advanced and impartial country in the world. Elementary education was obligatory and free right up to university level and Russia's universities were renowned for their high academic standards.

The people of all races in the Russian Empire had an equality of status and opportunity, which was un-parallel in the modern world.

On November 7, 1917, the Rothschild bankers fearful that replication of this freedom and prosperity would destroy their banking empire instigated and financed the revolution in Russia. The Russian Revolution led to a one-party dictatorship that was violent, bloody and vicious.

When Lenin died in 1924 and Stalin became the leader the Wall Street bankers were upset and have been fighting since to regain their turf. They targeted the Soviet Union as the enemy in the Cold War following World War II.

Russia experienced a rapid growth that was input-driven. Huge amounts of capital had been invested and a vast population mobilised to raise production, making rapid growth. After rapid growth they began experiencing declining increases in output. The law of diminishing returns took hold; the Soviet Union could not sustain its high economic output and eventually stagnated. Input-driven growth is limited as mere increases in input without an increase in the efficiency with those inputs are used it leads to diminishing returns.

Since the 1970's the Soviet Union experienced a long period of stagnation with their centrally planned economy, fixed prices, full employment and small income differences.

The reform policies did not work which led to the end of communism. The Soviet economy finally collapsed in 1989 which led to a complete overhaul of the economic system. Russia took responsibility for setting the USSR external debts although its population only made up half of the former USSR population.

The dissolution of the Warsaw Pact, defeating the Soviets and the eastern Block, the Soviet Union dismantled into 15 republics was not enough for the banking cartel. Sanctions have been imposed on the Russian economy by the US and its allies while cutting Russia's revenue through market manipulation.

Large parts of the economy that were previously in government hands were privatised as Russia made significant and stressful changes to move from a centrally planned economy to a more market based and global intergraded economy.

Austerity measures were imposed on them by the International Monetary Fund and the World Bank for financial assistance. It was shock therapy to force Russia to the ground so that they would fall apart.

The belt-tightening measures included eliminating food program subsidies, reducing wages, increasing corporate profits, and privatising public industries. This was to shrink the role of the state and soften the market for private investors.

It caused an economic collapse, a rapid decline in the value of their currency, a flight of foreign investment, millions plunged into poverty, income inequality increased rapidly and corruption and crime spread all over. Hyperinflation resulted from the removal of price controls.

The IMF blamed the hyperinflation on the government but the real culprit was the IMF's insistence on 'tight money'. As the economic collapse continued tax collection became increasingly difficult and the necessary capital was not made available for firms to modernise.

For six consecutive years Russia's GDP declined sharply, their output reduced by 40% until Russia adopted a stabilisation program to lower inflation. The main element of the stabilisation program was a currency peg which helped to keep the ruble stable.

When the Asia financial crisis hit the world Russia had let its currency go too high and held too few reserves.

The price of the Russian ruble dropped again in December 2014 as a consequence of the economic siege on the Russian Federation, the drop in global energy prices and speculation. This was all done to blame the Russian government and Vladimir Putin.

The objectives of the economic sanctions was not only to damage the trade ties and business between Russia and Europe but also to bring about economic instability in Russia and to create current instability and inflation. Instead of trying to stop the value of the ruble from dropping the Kremlin decided to invest strategically in Russian human capital.

Russia obtained permission from Turkey to build a gas pipeline Between Russia and Europe via Turkey. This pipe line would make the Turkish government an important energy corridor and the transit point, complete with transit revenues.

Russian business and trade ties have been redirected to the People's republic of China and East Asia for an important degree of economic and strategic insulation from the economic warfare being waged against them.

The US bankers want to establish control over the whole Russia, they want lordship and is not interested in cooperation. They want to divide Russia and control the abundant natural resources in Russian territory.

Two thirds of the Russian population have negative views about relations with Washington. The Russians are thinking of a response to expose and end US political domination and most importantly undermining US military-political power based on printing of dollars as a global currency.

Washington has taken on more than it can handle. The coming century will not be the 'American Century'.

Crisis of 1995: Mexico

Mexico was conquered in 1520 by the

Spanish General Cortes by the lure of gold. Mexico downfall in the twentieth century was due to the American and British oil companies fighting for the Mexican oil reserves. In the battle for ownership the Mexican government nationalised all foreign oil holdings for the next forty years.

When new oil reserves were discovered in the 1970's President Portillo undertook an impressive modernization and industrialization program, and Mexico became the most rapidly growing economy in the developing world.

This infuriated the powerful oil companies who were determined to sabotage Mexico's industrialization by securing rigid repayment of its foreign debt. President Portillo was aware of foreigners who were trying to destabilize the country but failed to stem the capital outflow.

To stabilize the situation the government took over the banks and compensated the private owners. Henry Kissinger's consulting firm was used to return the Mexican state-owned banks to private ownership. By 1994, Mexico had restored its standing with investors and the Mexican government was advised to unpeg and let the currency float to find its natural level.

They agreed, and the speculators pushed the peso down sharply collapsing the value. When Mexico banks ran out of dollars to pay off its creditors, the U.S. government stepped in with U.S. tax dollars but the money went straight into the vaults of Goldman Sachs, Morgan Stanley, and other big American lenders whose risky loans were on the line.

Mexico was propelled into a crippling national depression that lasted over a decade, with drastic cuts in government spending; sharp rise in sales taxes; at least one million layoffs; a spike in interest rates; and a collapse in consumer spending.

A lesson was learned; when big U.S. banks are threatened, the money will be found to protect them. The Mexican bailout taught managers of global banks that they couldn't lose.

Crisis of 1997: East Asia

In the Asian countries of Indonesia, Korea, Malaysia and the Philippines, a lot of successful companies, which had been surviving on their savings, decided to open up their financial markets to international capital in the early 1990's. The countries were doing well but decided they could do better if they borrowed a bit.

When they opened up to international capital they did not have the right regulatory laws in place or an understanding of the criteria of the lenders. They took a tremendous amount of short-term debt and often invested it in very good long-term projects.

By the middle of 1997 their creditors, mainly international banks realised the short-term debt was more than the short-term dollar assets and panic developed as they tried to be first to recover their money. All the creditors demanded their money all at once which led to the debtors to collapse as they were not able to come up with that amount in such a short period.

The currencies plummeted and interest rates soared. Working capital disappeared and production stopped. The whole region went into economic collapse. In Indonesia the crisis forced President Suharto, who reigned over the country for thirty-one years to accept a $43 billion loan from the IMF with tough conditions. The financial crisis resulted in chaos and the Indonesians youth under instruction attacked the Chinese shop owners and looted and torched their stores.

When the IMF intervened in the Asia crisis, it did it through provocative steps such as insisting on large scale closures of many banks and financial institutions in the region, they triggered a further panic making it much worse.

These countries had allowed their currencies to get too high and they had held too few reserves against them. The central banks then deliberately bought up foreign currency assets to keep their currencies weak and maintain a buffer of reserves. With this deliberate policy of reserve accumulation, Asian savings were made available to the American borrowers.

Crisis of 2001: Argentina

Before 1914 Argentina had experienced around fifty years of economic growth and was regarded as one of the richest counties in the world. The country was ruled by a small group of elite heavily invested in the agricultural export economy, but it was, not sustainable. Mounting political instability and armed revolts persuaded the Argentine elites to try to broaden the political system, but this led to the mobilisation of forces they could not control, and in 1930 came the first military coup.

Between then and 1983, Argentina oscillated backward and forward between dictatorship and democracy. There was a mass repression under military rule which peaked in the 1970s; with at least nine thousand people being illegally executed. Hundreds of thousands were also imprisoned and tortured.

During the periods of civilian rule there were elections; a democracy of sorts. Since the rise of Perón in the 1940s, democratic Argentina has been dominated by the political party he created, the *Partido Justicialista,* usually just called the Perónist Party. The Perónists won elections thanks to a huge political machine which succeeded by buying votes, dispensing patronage, and engaging in corruption. In a sense it was democracy, but it was not pluralistic as power was highly concentrated in the Party.

Perón had cultivated the labour movement as a political base. When it was weakened by military repression in the 1970s and 80s, his party simply switched to buying votes from others instead. Economic policies and institutions were designed to deliver income to their supporters, not to create a level playing field. Even the popularly elected government is quite able to override property rights and expropriate its own citizens with impunity.

A huge increase in the price of oil and years of excess of printing pesos Argentina went into hyperinflation. The idea was to generate an inflationary stampede to depreciate the debts of private firms, shatter the price controls in force since 1973, and especially benefits exporters through devaluation.

The economic chaos was welcomed by speculators who found that profiteering was a much safer way of making money than attempting to invest, increase productivity.

Argentina was targeted by international lenders with loans. To reduce the hyperinflation Carlos Menem adopted policies in 1989 to stabilise the economy. For a time the government was successful.

The crippling currency devaluations made it very difficult to repay its loans and the IMF stepped in. In 1991 the Argentina peso was tied to the U.S dollar. One peso was equal to one dollar by law.

The Argentina government and its central bank were prohibited by law from printing their own pesos, unless the pesos were fully backed by dollars held as foreign reserves.

The government persuaded people to open bank accounts in U.S dollars. The fixed currency policy caused exports to be very expensive and imports very cheap. Exports almost stopped while the people borrowed more money to increase their imports.

On December 1, 2001, the government froze all bank accounts, and a small amount of cash was only allowed for withdrawal from their peso accounts on a weekly basis. In January the devaluation was enacted, four pesos for one dollar. The government forcibly converted all the dollar bank accounts into pesos at the old one-for-one exchange rate. By doing this the government expropriated three-quarters of people's savings.

Argentina defied its creditors and simply walked away from its debts. By the fall of 2004, three years after a record default on a debt of more than $100 billion, the country was well on the road of recovery; and it had achieved this feat without foreign help.

Crisis of 2008: Global

The only surprise about the economic crisis of 2008 was that it came as a surprise to so many. For a few observers, it was a textbook case that was not only predictable but also predicted.

In the 1980's the savings and loan industry collapsed after interest was raised to unprecedented levels. After the crises the Fed reacted to a stock market crisis by lowering interest rates, making investment money readily available, inflating the stock market to unprecedented heights in the 1990's.

The investment world went mad. Millions upon millions of investors ignored time-honoured principles for investing in stocks, such as due diligence and fundamental analysis, they began to buy and sell purely out of emotion. Believing in the wonders of technology, they rushed to buy technology and Internet stocks like rats following a Wall Street pied piper.

The investors were convinced that 'this time it would be different' – that the tech bubble was not a false mania, like the South Sea Bubble or the late 1920's. It was the real thing. Debt did not matter as long as the company had innovative technology ideas, or could sell products from a Web site, its stock was sure to make investors rich.

What the majority of investors had forgotten, or perhaps never stopped to think about was the victims of past speculative manias that had been just as certain of becoming rich.

Under pressure from the Clinton Administration Fannie Mae, the U.S.'s biggest mortgagee provided riskier mortgage loans to less creditworthy borrowers. This was in line with the U.S. Government policy from 1970 onwards which emphasized deregulation to encourage business. These policies resulted in less regulation and disclosure of information about new activities undertaken by banks and financial institutions.

Before the late 1970's there were two principal forms of mortgage lending. The lender could issue a mortgage loan and keep it; or the lender could sell the loan to Fannie Mae, allowing the bank to make a third loan, and so on. In 1979-81 policy changes were made that would flood the housing market with even more money.

To get people in more debt, they used the bait of home ownership and the promise of ready cash from home equity loans. As mortgages became more available, house prices began to rise which led to a housing construction boom and facilitated debt-financed consumer spending.

When the "prime" market was exhausted lenders resorted to riskier "sub-prime" market for new borrowers and fanned the housing market with a series of high-risk changes in mortgage instruments. Purchasers were lulled by easy payments not even covering the initial interest rates. These homeowners were gambling that either their incomes would increase to meet the payment burden or that the housing market would continue to go up.

Loans of various types (e.g., mortgages, credit card and automobiles) were easy to obtain and consumers assumed an unprecedented debt load. Americans received credit cards in their mail, and shopping became the national sport.

Credit cards play directly into the tendency to treat money differently because they seemed to devalue the dollar. As they seem to devalue the dollar, credit cards cause people to spend money that they might not ordinaryly spend, leading to credit card abuse.

The middle class celebrated their newfound wealth by dinning in fancy restaurants, dressing in designer clothes, driving luxury cars, and living in mansions-all financed by debt.

It caused the greatest boom which was caused by debt, not money; by inflation not production; by borrowing, not working. It was money for nothing because money was nothing.

The number of financial agreements and collateral debt obligations greatly increase as the total U.S. mortgage debt increased by over 80% between 1991 and 2001, while the residential debt grew another 50% between 2001 and 2005. Homeowners took equity out of their homes through home sales, refinancing and home equity loans.

From 2000 to 2003, the Federal Reserve lowered the rates from 6.5% to 1% to soften the collapse of the dot-com bubble and the September 11 terrorist attacks, as well as to combat a perceived risk of deflation. Further downward pressures on interest rates were created by the high and rising U.S. current account deficit.

The mortgage banks off-loaded their risk by slicing the mortgages and selling them to investors as "mortgage-backed securities".

Fannie Mae devised a new method of extracting money from the markets. It took the securities and pooled them again into an instrument called a Real Estate Mortgage Conduit (REMIC). As all these risks multiply they generate new forms of danger which, are typically underestimated by the investors taking the risks.

Freeman wrote REMIC's are very complex derivatives as they are pure bets sold to institutional investors and individuals, to draw money into the housing bubble. Most of these REMIC's were just very risky obligations.

The recession had been triggered by a sharp nationwide drop in the U.S. housing prices that had caused the market in 'sub-prime' –very risky- mortgage loans to collapse. When the market determined that houses were no longer such a super investment many people defaulted. The result was a glut of unsold houses and a drastic reduction in the amount of home building.

The Bush administration at first denied there was any serious problem. We had just built a few too many houses, the president suggested. In the early months of the crisis, the Treasury and the Federal Reserve veered like drunk drivers from one course to another, saving some banks while letting others go down. It was impossible to discern the principles behind their decision making. Bush administration officials argued that they were being pragmatic.

Then the U.S. administration applied pressure on Reserve Banks all over the world ensuring they regulated anti-money laundering and counter-terrorist financing. The first signs they saw of international calamity had nothing to do with laundering or terrorist financing; the trigger was 'sub-prime' lending.

Two mortgage hedge funds owned by the investment bank Bear Stearns went broke in 2007, along with the American home Mortgage Corporation and three investment funds owned by the French bank BNP Paribas.

The recession was overtaken by a financial crisis in March 2008, when Bear Stearns itself collapsed. The crisis became acute with the bankruptcy of Lehman Brothers, and the distress sale of Merrill Lynch.

When the U.S. loans went into their inevitable default Fannie Mae was responsible for the debt as it guaranteed payment of interest and principal in the event of default. Fannie Mae went bankrupt and the hedge funds, pension funds and other institutions suffered losses. It cost the U.S. government $5.4 trillion when Fannie Mae and Freddie Mac were taken into receivership.

The BBC revealed that Northern Rock

could not refinance fast enough and had been granted emergency lending support from the Bank of England. The effect on the British public was electric; immediately the Bank's electronic website was deluged with withdrawal requests, it soon crashed. The next day depositors formed queues in the high streets, withdrawing £2 billion. This was the biggest run on a British bank for over a century and the crippled bank had to be nationalised. To all around the world, this was a salutary reminder that old-fashioned bank runs can still happen.

The 2008 Global Financial crisis is considered by many economists the worst financial crises since the Great Depression of the 1930's.

The secret of Wall Street was out, the derivatives were not real or secure assets. The $680 trillion derivative bubble was an illusion and panic spread around the world as an increasing number of investment banks had to prevent "runs" on their hedge funds by refusing withdrawals from nervous customers.

Stock markets went into free fall as trillions of dollars of fictitious wealth were wiped out. Silence descended over the global commerce as international trade froze, and ships stood empty near ports around the world because banks would no longer issue letters of credit. Factories shut down as millions of workers were laid off as commercial paper and money market funds used to pay wages froze.

Major banks in the U.S. and the UK, were literally hours away from shutting down and ATM's were on the verge of running out of cash. The world was threatened with a big deflationary collapse.

At the height of the Western financial crisis, the G20 leaders met in London in April 2009 to try and rescue the global economy and succeeded. By doing this they demonstrated that global institutions and procedures are needed to deal with a rising tide of global challenges, caused by central banks.

The central banks stepped in. There was enough money but the 'sub-prime' borrowers defaulted and investors did not want to invest in CDO.

The U.S. Federal Reserve and the central banks of Europe, Canada, Australia and Japan saved the troubled banks by providing the troubled banks with $315 billion in credit.

The recession caused less spending and a liquidity crush causing many firms short of cash. Demand was down and firms fired their less productive workers who struggled to obtain new low paid jobs. Many of them may now be permanently unemployable. There is no longer a steady, secure life somewhere in the middle.

By getting rid of the less productive

workers the per-labour-hour productivity rose dramatically. The reduction of middle class was permanent as many workers had been over employed relative to their skills.

The burst of the housing bubble and the financial crisis meant that people lost a lot of wealth. People suddenly had to focus on their finances and change their spending habits.

When placed under pressure Alan Greenspan the retired chairman of the Federal Reserve had to admit that he had made a mistake and found a flaw in the model that he perceived as the critical functioning structure that defines how the world works.

It is very comforting to know that after each economic crash an impressive number of so-called market experts, financial experts and economists brainstorm and theorize about what caused the crash and what sort of measures would help prevent another disaster.

Libya and the Arab uprising

From 1551 to 1911 Libya was ruled by the Ottoman Empire, by Italy from 1911 to 1943 and from 1943 to 1951 was under the military suzerainty of Britain and France. The central Bank of Libya was founded in 1956 and was run as a typical central bank until the bloodless *coup d'etat* of September 1, 1969.

André Klopper

Oil of an exceptionally high quality was discovered in 1959, but King Idris al Mahdi as-Sanusi failed to capitalise on this and the bulk of the oil profits went to the foreign oil companies.

On assuming power in 1969 Mu'ammar Muhammad al-Qathafi took control of most of the economic activities in the country. He was described by the mainstream media as being a terrible dictator and a blood sucking monster, but the reality was that with the exception of the city of Benghazi he had the support of 90% of the population.

He was very popular for he provided the following for free; education, electricity, health care and housing. The wealth of the country was fairly distributed to all the population of 5.79 million.

Another major achievement, which Qathafi initiated was the conversion of the Nubian Sandstone Fossil Aquifer System into the Great Man-Made River, which supplies 6,500,000 cubic meters of fresh water daily to the cities of Tripoli, Sirte and Benghazi. The extracted water is ten times cheaper than desalinated water. The whole project was financed without a single foreign loan.

Then why did NATO intervene on pretext of fabricated human right abuses? Since 1971 when the US abandoned the gold standard for the petrodollar any attempt the displace the US dollar as premier reserve currency has been blocked and opposed with violence.

In November 2000 Saddam Hussein of Iraq decreed that all oil payments would be in future be made in euros, as he did not wish to deal in the currency of the enemy. As has already been proven, the possession of weapons of mass destruction pretext was a deliberate concocted hoax and it was this currency decision, which cost Saddam Hussein his life and the destruction of his country.

In similar circumstances Qathafi announced in 2010 the creation of gold dinar as a replacement for the settlement of all foreign transactions in a proposed region of over 200 million people. Libya at that time possessed 144 tons of gold. His intention was not to return to the gold standard but a new unit of account with oil exports and thus crossed a red line and paid the ultimate price.

In January 2011 we were informed by the main media about a 'spontaneous' uprising sweeping North Africa and the Middle East. The truth however, is that the uprising were part of an immense geopolitical campaign conceived in the West and carried out through proxies with the assistance of foundations and organisations throughout the world.

The Youth Movements received training

and support from various corporate and US government sponsors. The activists returned to their countries to sow unrest in a region-wide coordinated campaign. This was proved beyond a doubt when Iraq's army had shot down two British aircraft as they were carrying weapons for ISIL (ISIS) terrorists in Al Anbar province.

The fires caused by these uprising are still burning in Iraq, Libya, Egypt and Syria.

World economy after 2008

The world economy is just as vulnerable to a financial crisis as it was in 2007, with the added danger that debt ratios are now far higher. The disturbing fact is that China, Brazil, Turkey and other emerging economies have succumbed to private credit booms of their own.

The prolonged monetary stimulus in the U.S., Europe, and Japan has led to a leakage of liquidity, contaminating the rest of the world. Emerging markets have racked up U.S.$2 trillion in foreign debt since 2008. The rising powers of Asia are therefore no longer able to act as a firebreak as they did after the Lehman crash; as they may themselves now be a source of risk.

The world economy is in many ways more fragile now than in the build-up to the Lehman crisis.

Most economists, when explaining unemployment cite the Keynesian, neo-monetarist, and "aggregate demand" stories that there is not enough spending in the economy. In the 2008 crises after the collapse of the housing bubble, asset prices were lower, indebtedness was higher, and people were more uncertain about the future. Most people cut back on their expenditure; this led to lower sales, lower output and eventually lower employment. The Keynesian explanation makes sense, but it doesn't explain the longer-run trends.

The more the economy recovered from the recession it became clearer that significant structural changes had taken place. With greater spending and stronger aggregate demand as the Keynesians and other economists advocate; most people who were laid off during the recession would have found jobs by now.

The new jobs did not look like the old jobs because business had already rebuilt under the assumption that those old jobs were not coming back. When the economy picked up the brute force labour was very much in demand. The retrenched middle management level however stayed unemployed.

Another factor is the growing costs of

employing people, medical costs, pension costs and higher risk of lawsuits. Machines which produce a lot of goods and services very cheaply are more and more able to replace cheap manual labour.

27. Currency Wars

There are a number of things which will set off the global financial avalanche which can't be predicted in advance. These are; a broad Middle East war that could send the price of oil soaring; the euro zone could begin to fragment; a major bank's derivatives book could blow up; interest rates could spike, setting off a death spiral in government finances; or the implosion of the leveraged speculating community. The list goes on.

Whatever the proximate cause, the bursting of this latest, greatest bubble, will lead to the mass-realisation that un-backed fiat currency, created in unlimited quantities by over-indebted governments, will cause inflation to spread. After the bust the world will return to some form of sound money.

The first currency war was in 1930 when the major countries abandoned the gold standard. The countries were fighting deflation and trying to revive growth during the Great Depression. The currency war was a temporary and necessary measure to fight the deflationary aspects of the gold standard.

Britain was the first to take itself off the gold standard and the pound immediately fell 30 percent against the U.S. dollar. There were about 25 countries with close economic or imperial links to Britain that had tied their currencies to the sterling; the shock waves of devaluation extended around the world.

One country after another left the gold standard and completely devalued their currencies as they tried to jumpstart their economies. They also put up trade barriers and tariffs to protect their local industries.

The problem was all the countries did the same and all of them were worse off.

The second currency war happened in the 1970's when President Nixon ended the link between the dollar and the price of gold. For more than a decade the U.S. government had created more money than it should have. Very high oil prices and high prices for food caused a vicious cycle as workers demanded higher wages because they expected high inflation.

As the U.S. government ran budget and trade deficits, foreign central banks began to demand more and more gold in exchange for dollars they held. The U.S. gold reserves kept falling and Nixon pulled the plug and introduced a 10 percent surcharge on imports.

Most of the countries were trying to rid themselves of the constraints of a fixed exchange rate system so governments could spend freely. A month after Nixon's move Japan floated its currency and many other countries followed suit. Just as in the 1930's, currency devaluations in the 1970's also came with trade barriers. The result was higher inflation, higher unemployment, and no real benefits to anyone.

At the moment the U.S dollar's privileged reserve currency status is mitigating the risk of America's debt crisis. It enables them to carry a current debt load that cannot be sustained indefinitely. The IMF is currently using their Special Drawing Rights (SDR) a currency-basket for their transactions with shareholder governments. The SDR basket comprises the dollar, the euro, the Japanese yen, and the British pound.

Currency wars are fought globally in all major financial centres at once, twenty-four hours per day, by bankers, traders, politicians and automated systems; the fate of economies and their affected citizens hang in the balance.

The third currency war is about to begin. Every country wants to grow its way out of debt and for most it means increasing exports. If they decrease the value of their currency they will become more competitive. However, as seen in the previous two currencies wars, if everyone does the same no one wins. Japan has started the war when it devalued their yen. When will the other countries start to follow suit?

The CEO of Fortress Paper which produces the security paper used in around 10 percent of all euro banknotes and in a dozen other currencies said it typically takes up to four years to design, manufacture, print, distribute, and circulate a new currency. Governments need that time to come up with banknotes that can't be easily counterfeited by the high-tech organised crime syndicates that are by now well ahead of the technology that was used for the euro zone's previous national currencies before 1999.

28. Oil Reserves

Energy is a requirement of complex societies and essential to wealth. The more complex the society, the more energy flow it needs. Therefore oil is very important for our civilization to continue to prosper. There is a small minority who sees the oil crisis unfolding. It's clear for those who know that the media wants us to believe in an underestimated future demand for oil and an overestimated potential supply.

Most authorities continue to reassure the public that today's soaring energy prices are temporary, that oil reserves are virtually limitless, and that production will outpace demand for the remainder of our lives. This is an outright contradiction of facts.

The trends for the last thirty years show declining returns from oil exploration, peaking or declining oil production everywhere but in a few OPEC nations. This is while the world is experiencing an increasing demand for energy, especially among the world's largest developing nations.

Data seems to indicate that we have at least reached a declining reliance on fossil fuels and possibly for some raw materials. A new energy subsidy is needed if a declining standard of living and a future global collapse are to be adverted.

The energy production is a problem that cannot be solved with a quick infusion of cash. Solving it will take not only massive amounts of money but also many years of work developing alternatives. Failing to solve it could spell disaster for the population on earth.

In 1973, because of the Arab-Israeli war,

Things You Should Know

OPEC imposed an embargo on oil exports. This caused higher fuel prices which resulted in a worldwide economic slowdown and a lower demand for oil, which brought oil prices down.

Since 1973 and the founding of OPEC, the price of oil has been an important leading indicator of both the U.S. economy and the stock market. Over the past thirty years, the United States has been losing control of its energy supply, and as a result their economy has grown increasingly vulnerable to external political and economic factors.

Between 1970 and 1982, oil prices went from $1.35 a barrel to a high of nearly $35 a barrel, a twenty-six-fold increase.

Thirty five percent of the world population were living in China and India, yet the per capita consumption energy for China and India was a fraction of what the developed world used. In the past decade China and India's economies have grown to the point where it consumes nearly 90% as many goods and services as does the United States. These countries will within this decade surpass the oil consumption of the United States.

According to the U.S Geological Survey global discovery of large new oil fields peaked in 1962 and has been declining ever since. The largest 1% of oil fields contains 75% of all the discovered oil and the largest 3% contains 94% of the oil. The implication of this skewed distribution is that as exploration progresses, the average size of the fields discovered decreases. This is why it's so much harder to maintain production in the declining stages than in the growing phase of the oil industry.

Very soon the global oil production will enter a permanent decline, and with the ever increasing demand for it, the oil prices are going to skyrocket causing a crisis of epic proportions.

A common argument today is that new technologies will save us from the threat of an oil crisis, by increasing oil or make us less dependent on oil. The earth's crust contains only so much oil that can be extracted for a reasonable cost, and no amount of money or brains can change that fact.

We are more vulnerable to an energy shortfall today than we ever were; therefore an energy crisis will be the biggest problem our civilisation has ever faced.

One option is that the scale of all human enterprises must contract with the energy supply. We have to conduct our activities of daily life on a smaller scale, whether we like it or not, and the only intelligent course of action is to prepare for it.

Producing food will become a problem of supreme urgency. People will have to move into small towns and farms and do labour-intensive farming.

Another option is that one assumes our leaders are a little more farsighted and are planning our civilisation more towards a level of complexity that matches our long-term, sustainable energy production. Improving product design and ensuring products that last longer, are also easy to repair, rather than higher consumption. What about a limit on population growth?

U.S. oil output has been declining until shale gas production boomed recently. Shale gas has risen from 2% of domestic production a decade ago to 37% of supply and prices dropped dramatically by 2008.

Wall Street bankers and their "market analysis" gave an upbeat projection of the role of shale gas and oil making the western hemisphere self-sufficient in energy by 2030.

It is becoming increasingly clear however that the shale revolution is a short-term flash in the energy pan.

To extract the shale gas, a hydraulic fracture is formed by pumping a fracturing fluid into the well bore at sufficient pressure to cause the porous shale rock strata to crack. The toxic fracture fluid continues further into the rock extending the crack.

The oil and gas industry is the only one that is allowed to inject known hazardous materials unchecked directly into or adjacent to underground drinking water supplies.

Secrecy shrouding the fracking process and the Bush-era loopholes obscured consumer knowledge of food safety. Two major agricultural insurance companies refuse to cover damages from fracking.

Ranches in Pennsylvania, North Dakota, Louisiana and New Mexico have been reporting health problems and incidents of dead and tainted livestock due to elevated levels of contaminants from nearby wells.

Although the OPEC nations are producing around 30 million barrels a day, the same as what they did thirty years ago, they are experiencing a decline in their oil reserves. They are regularly pumping up to 80% water out of their oil wells and their internal pressures are dissipating. The Saudis are suffering from lost oil surplus, rising government debt, higher domestic energy and food costs.

The OPEC nations have become a group of disorganised and devious dealers who discount prices and lie about output on a regular basis. The cartel has no unity any more, and the justification for the petrodollar and the banking system based on the U.S. Treasury bonds is disintegrating.

The resources on this planet is finite. We are quite literally consuming our precious planet until there will come a day when there is nothing of any worth left of it. We're not just biting the hand that feeds us- we're eating it alive.

29. Facts And Figures

a) Concept of large numbers

70% of the population would be able to tell how many zero's there are in a million, billion, a trillion and a quadrillion, but only 10% would grasp the true value. A million seconds is twelve days, a billion seconds is almost 34 years, a trillion is 34,000 years, and a quadrillion is 34 million years.

Keep this in mind when reading the facts and figures.

b) World GDP

During the Great Depression U.S. GDP fell

by about 25%

During the last crisis Mexico's GDP fell 22%, Japan 15.2% and Germany 14.4%

The current GDP of the entire world is about $60 trillion

c) U.S. GDP

Year	GDP	Government spending
2007	$14 Trn	$163 Bn
2010	$14.6 Trn	$1.4 Trn

d) U.S. house prices

From 1916 to 1921 U.S. house prices fell 30%

Between 2001 and 2006 U.S. house prices went up on average by 80% while income only rose by 2%. This indicated a bubble which burst in 2007 when house prices fell below 50% for the first time since 1945.

e) U.S. Government revenue and debt

| Date | Debt |

1950	$19 billion
1980	$350 Billion
1984	$3 Trillion
2011	$15 Trillion
2014	$17.25 Trillion
2016	$19.0 Trillion

It is clear that the U.S. government debt has skyrocketed since 1984.

During 2011 more than 40% of U.S. government expenses were funded with borrowed money.

36% of loans have a maturity of less than one year

64% of loans have a 2 to 30 year maturity with an average maturity of 4.3 years.

Most people assume there is no credit limit and the government can keep borrowing forever at record low interest rates.

Debt ceiling is NOT the credit ceiling and can be raised by congress at any time.

Looking at the context of above table do you believe the U.S. government has their finance under control or that a Ponzi scheme is going to bust?

In the United States during the 1980s $2.37 of private debt were required to produce $1 of growth in GDP, in the 1990s this figure rose to $2.99, and in the 2000s there was a dramatic increase to $5.67 for each incremental dollar of growth- a level which will soon become untenable.

f) U.S; States and Municipal pension funds

According to a 2009 study of 116 state pension schemes conducted by Robert Novy-Marx and Joshua Rauh, the total amount of assets in those funds was $1.94 trillion. The total reported liabilities were $2.98 trillion, a shortfall of over a trillion dollars. By using proper accounting methods, Norvy-Marx and Rauh calculated the true value of state and municipal pension liability at $5.2 trillion. It is a fraud committed on state employees, whose pension plans aren't properly funded.

g) Dow Jones Industrial average

From 1928 to 1981 the Dow rose by three times.

Between 1982 and 2009 the Dow rose by 14 times.

h) Financial assets

From 1960 to 1985 U.S. financial assets were 4 time the size of GDP.

From 1985 to 2000 U.S. financial assets grew to 10 times the size of GDP.

Things You Should Know

i) U.S. household debt

Date	Total debt	Debt as % of disposable income
1989	$13 Trillion	75%
2012	$58 Trillion	120%

From 1989 to 2012 the median U.S. income remained at $51,000

Stagnated living standards, rising unemployment, higher debt, larger retirement population and growing defence budget. ($13 trillion mortgage debt in 2012)

j) U.S. interest rates

For the last nine years the interest rates in the U.S. was close to 0% causing the massive housing and stock market bubbles.

k) U.S. unemployment

Between 1950 and 1973 the unemployment rate was 4.2%.

Between 1973 and 1993 the unemployment rate was 6.7%.

Although the U.S. government altered the unemployment figure the real figure is 25% unemployed

l) Bailouts

In the 1980's the U.S. government bailouts were in the millions. By the 1990's they were in the billions, today they are in the trillions. The problem is that the crisis is getting bigger, not diminishing as some would hope.

m) Derivatives

Year	Amount in trillion
1998	$75
2002	$200
2006	$415
2007	$520
2012	$1,000

In 2013 it was $1,200,000,000,000,000 or if you prefer $1,200 trillion

Bank	Assets	Derivatives
JPMorgan Chase	$1.8 trn	$69 trn
Bank of America	$1.4 trn	$44 trn
Goldman Sachs	$114 bn	$41 trn

Why is this not front-page news? Because

banks and hedge funds are frequently on both sides of these bets, and they net out long and short derivatives positions to arrive at a modest-sounding exposure number. The fact is that actual risk does indeed rise along with total amount of derivatives.

The global derivatives markets are unstable and can bring about catastrophic failure. A threat of failure to any of the major banks is an immediate threat to the others. The network topology where the very high percentage of exposures is concentrated among a few highly interconnected banks implies that they will stand and fail together. These derivatives are financial weapons of mass destruction.

n) America's oil reserves

Year	Spare oil capacity
1985	8.7 million barrels a day
2012	Almost none

o) China's properties

While America declines and Europe convulses, China's huge cities are being constructed at breakneck speed, complete with brand-new high-rise condominiums, office buildings, and infrastructure such as roads and bridges. China's urban population is currently 500 million.

Leslie Stahl noted in 2013, "We

discovered that the most populated nation is building houses, districts and cities with no one in them... desolate condos and vacant subdivisions uninhabited for miles and miles."

Construction is far outpacing projected demand. In 2012, unsold apartments increased by 40 percent, as measured by floor space. What is happening in China is a housing bubble, even worse than the one America had experienced.

Shanghai's apartment prices rose more than 1.5 times between 2003 and 2010. This is mainly due to the huge inflow of money. Capital controls prevent profits from being invested overseas and because of low banking interest the surplus money flows into property.

The average price of apartments in Beijing is 57 times the average worker's annual income.

65 million houses in 660 cities across China are vacant.

Monthly increase in property prices in 2010 were between 5 and 10% monthly in the major cities across China

p) World property bubbles

Country	Overvalued %
China	20
Netherlands	20
Spain	20
UK	20
Sweden	30

New Zealand	35
Australia	42
Singapore	50
Hong Kong	70
Canada	75

q) Increase in debt of some countries from 2007 to 2012

Australia	369%
France	132%
Germany	124%
Ireland	219%
Italy	113%
Japan	124%
Russia	231%
Spain	181%
UK	197%
U.S.	147%

In today's global economy these are scarce:

1. Quality land and natural resources
2. Intellectual property and good ideas about what should be produced.
3. Quality labour with unique skills.

Here is what are not scarce these days:

1. Unskilled labour as more countries join the global economy.
2. Money in the bank or held in government

securities.

30. Wall Street

In 1947 finance and insurance contributed 2.4% of the U.S. GDP. By the late 1970's finance and insurance contributed 4.7% of the total economic output of which Wall Street accounted for 0.34%. Wall Street made a few people rich, raised some capital and made some markets.

By the early 1990's the finance industry as a whole was generating over 6.5% of economic output while Wall Street's share of GDP had tripled to 1%. No other industry had grown at that rate, none at all.

The turbocharged growth was fuelled by two ingredients; the dismantling of international controls on the movement of capital allowing Wall Street to gain a little from the vast volume of money as it passed on through.

Secondly, massive growth in the derivatives market providing large fees for Wall Street. This is reflected in the 30% of "ALL" profits in the U.S. economy that were made either on Wall Street or in insurance. The 30% profit is obtained from a sector that only

Things You Should Know

contributes 4.3% of the U.S. economy output.

The small hedge fund business had become a booming multi-billion–dollar industry. The types of funds were astonishingly diverse: macro, micro, global, quant. In this new age, running money came to be the ultimate goal for the trader.

The government had no idea how the Wall Street actually operated. The ineptitude of the regulators was an open joke. Laws were broken so often and with such impunity, that there were effectively no rules.

What started the Wall Street bubble? It began with too much excess. First there were all the corporate executives and investment bankers, who made millions of dollars making terrible business mistakes which destroyed the value of their companies.

The government bailed out their companies, while the executives kept all the money they made from making the decisions that destroyed their companies, and they were even rewarded with handsome bonuses. Why? The government could always borrow so much money, it really didn't matter.

Why? The stock the government bought just kept going up along with the rest of the stock market, despite terrible management.

André Klopper

The Wall Street traders believed they were the unfortunate victims of a once-in-a-thousand-year storm. The crisis was not something that just happened to the financial markets; it was man-made-it was something that Wall Street did to itself and to the rest of the world.

For those who don't by the "it just happened" argument, Wall Street advocates have others. The government made us do it, through its encouragement of homeownership and lending to the poor. Or, the government should have stopped us from doing it; it was the fault of the regulators.

The Wall Street secrets were gradually revealed in their entire sly splendour.

The Wall Street Ponzi scheme collapse came on 15 September 2008 when Lehman Brothers filed for bankruptcy. The people were horrified when they read about it and other horror stories such as General Motors that went bust, Goldman Sachs seeking emergency funding, Citygroup crippled and AIG and Merrill Lynch in crises.

Across the world, the story was the same. The British government acquired most of the stock in the Royal Bank of Scotland (RBS) and further holdings in various other institutions, accumulating debts equal to the UK's GDP. The Irish government undertook to guarantee its bank debt, thereby destroying its own creditworthiness.

It was a heck of crises and we are slowly picking our way out of the mess as governments stepped in preventing the collapse of the entire global financial system.

Although there is still risk; the monetary policy needs to be loose to prevent deflation, house prices began climbing and financial sectors are becoming profitable again.

The Wall Street Ponzi scheme is propped up by the Fed printing money, and around the world governments "you the taxpayer" are facing the collapse of capitalism, a system no longer able to pay its way.

The world has far too much debt that it can't pay back in the normal way. Debt however can go away via the following methods;

1. Defaults that are painful and no one wants them.

2. Paying down debt through economic growth which is almost impossible

3. Eroding the burden of debt through inflation or currency devaluations. This is the only viable option to the Western leaders.

Every central bank is trying to get things

right, the Bank of England has devalued the pound to improve exports by allowing creeping inflation and keeping interest rates at zero.

The Fed has tried to weaken the dollar to boost manufacturing and exports. The Bank of Japan is now trying to radically depreciate the yen. However, countries like Brazil, Russia, China, Malaysia and Indonesia will not sit idly by while the developed central banks weaken their currencies; they too are fighting to keep their currencies from appreciating.

There is a difference between borrowing money for infrastructure; spending that will benefit our children and the borrowing of money to spend on ourselves today, with no future benefits.

31. Collapse

Collapse is fast becoming the elephant in the room as it is a socially awkward subject. Only serious people discuss it in hushed tones to their intimate friends. They don't discuss it with colleagues, for dwelling on the topic of collapse is not conducive to furthering their careers.

Social inertia is an awesome force and many people are almost genetically predisposed to not want to understand that collapse is inevitable. Many others understand this truth on some level but refuse to act on it.

Collapse is like a flood that inundates the lowlands first, then reaches the higher grounds and washes away the hills, it eventually reaches everybody and just as in a real flood, what makes survival possible is cooperation, not competition.

During its early stages, collapse affects the most vulnerable: the poorest, least protected, least privileged communities, families and individuals.

People who see collapse as a lofty pursuit for themselves and a dire experience for those who are less capable and less prepared, simply need to wait their turn – "then they too will be humbled."

Bubble; an asset class is in a bubble when;

a) Its price rises far beyond what rational analysis would have deemed reasonable just a few years before.

b) Individuals making money doing things experts used to find difficult.

c) Tried-and true business practices are replaced with 'innovations' that are scams.

d) They can be identified fairly early in their life-cycles, but tend to go on longer than reasonable analysts expect.

e) As a bubble forms, a unique mantra emerges to justify its excesses.

Today's fiat currencies meet the above criteria. Bubbles have one trait; they usually go out with a bang. Virtually every major bubble in financial history has popped rather than deflated gradually. This Money Bubble, as the biggest of them all, will put its predecessors to shame.

Bubbles always burst and they almost always go back to where they started or a bit lower.

The earth's finite endowment of fossil fuels, metal ores, other industrial and agricultural inputs, fresh water and fertile soil are either past their all-time peak of production or will soon achieve it.

Based on Glugston's projections, the increasing scarcity of the non-renewable resources required to maintain industrial civilisation will most certainly trigger a social collapse by mid- century.

Most of the people however do not wish to discuss the global meltdown. They think as the resources begin to run out a slow and steady deterioration would follow which could continue for centuries without reaching any conclusive historical endpoint.

As the world economy expands, so does the highways and bridges, the oil terminals, refineries and pipelines, the airports, seaports, electrical grid and so on. As the economy expands, all of these have to expand alongside it, to maintain and reserve capacity to avoid bottlenecks, shortages, traffic jams and blackouts.

When resource scarcity forces the economy to start contracting, the infrastructure cannot contract with it, because they have all been built to a certain scale that cannot be reduced retroactively. The infrastructures have been designed to be efficient and realize economies of scale only when utilized at close to full capacity. Even as they are used less, their maintenance cost remains the same, swallowing up an ever-larger proportion of the economy. At some point they would just cease to function at all.

The phenomenon of marginal returns produces an arc that rises nicely at first, then flattens out, and then declines. In his thesis, The Collapse of Complex Societies Tainter finds the familiar arc of marginal returns mirrors the arc of the rise, decline and fall of civilisations.

In the beginning of a civilisation, returns to investment in complexity, are extremely high. Over time and with increasing complexity, returns on investment in society begin to level off and turn negative.

He had analysed the collapse of twenty-seven separate civilisations over a 4,500-year period. He considered an enormous range of possible factors explaining collapse, including resource depletion, natural disasters, invasions, economic distress, social dysfunction, religion and bureaucratic incompetence. Civilisations are complex systems and as the complexity of society increases, the inputs needed to maintain society increase exponentially.

Not only do inputs increase exponentially with the scale of civilisation, but the outputs of civilisation and governments decline per unit of input when measured in terms of public goods and services provided. It is the law of diminishing returns. In effect, society asks its members to pay progressively more in taxes and they get progressively less in government services.

Bureaucracies that started out as efficient organisations turn into inefficient obstacles to improvement, more concerned with their own perpetuation than with service to society.

Elites who manage the institutions of society slowly become more concerned with their own share of a shrinking pie than with the welfare of the society as a whole. They go from leading to leeching. America has reached the point of negative return.

More traditional historians have pointed to factors such as earthquakes, droughts or barbarian invasions, but Tainter shows that civilisations that were finally brought down by barbarians had repelled barbarians many times before and civilisations that were destroyed by earthquakes had re-built from earthquakes many times before. What matters in the end is not the invasion or earthquake, but the response.

Societies that are not overtaxed or overburdened can respond vigorously to a crisis and rebuild after a disaster, while those that that are overtaxed and overburdened may simply give up.

Tainter makes one additional point that is particularly relevant to twenty-first-century society. There is a difference between whole civilisation collapse and the collapse of individual societies or nations within a civilisation. When Rome fell, the whole civilisation collapsed because there was no independent society to take its place. European civilization did not collapse again after the 6th century because for every state that collapsed there was another state to fill the void.

In his view, "Collapse, if and when it comes again, will be global. No longer can any individual nation collapse. World civilisation will disintegrate as a whole."

At some point productivity and taxation can no longer sustain society, and elites attempt to cheat the input process with credit, leverage, debasement and all other forms. These methods work for a brief period before the illusion of debt-fuelled growth is overtaken by the reality of lost wealth amid growing income inequality.

At that point society has three choices: simplification, conquest or collapse. Simplification is a voluntary effort to reduce society's expectations and return the input-output ratio to a more sustainable and productive level.

Conquest is the effort to take resources from neighbours by force in order to provide new inputs.

Collapse is a sudden, involuntary and chaotic form of simplification.

What I have given you thus far is an analysis of the flaws in the running of the world-wide financial system and the global economy, which suggest the mending that needs to be done. The clean-up will take years and there is no quick fix, so you need to brace yourself for perhaps a decade of economic stagnation.

The world will not come to an end but while

the West struggles to get out of debt, the strong inner resilience of Western societies will come through, in one way or another.

Survivors of disasters share several common traits. A certain degree of indifference or detachment is definitely helpful, including indifference to suffering. The most important characteristic is the will to survive. Next are the self-reliance and the sheer stubborn inability to surrender in the face of seemingly insurmountable odds, opposing opinions from anyone else.

Like most great civilisations, America has a strong belief in their permanence. They are confident in their ability to survive any challenge, and they believe their values and ideals are superior. Naturally, they want their civilisation to continue well into the future. They have a vested interest in it.

Yet an objective view of history tells us that there really are no guarantees. We know that civilizations collapse regularly. Over the past hundred years, the United States has successfully pulled through a number of close brushes with disaster.

André Klopper

32. Hyperinflation or Deflation?

Most people belief that the government is destroying their life and their currency over time with inflation. They will study charts which show how the value of their currency had declined over the last hundred years.

However, inflation over the long term correlated with rising standard of living. Inflation rises during times when population is growing, urbanisation is rising, empires are being built, and the most powerful new technologies are advancing into the mainstream.

Technologies and greater urbanisation allow us to create progress through a simple concept called specialisation of labour. The more we focus on what we do best and develop specialised skills in that area, the more productive we become and the more we can afford to have others specialise as well.

Depreciating currencies almost always generates higher inflation down the line. The fight between inflation and deflation is a tug of war. At first in the 1930's deflation was winning the tug of war, but devaluations and money printing stopped deflation in its tracks. In the 1970's there was no need for devaluations, loose money, and inflation cut the value of the dollar in half.

Our financial crisis is caused by too much debt. At the moment with the low interest world-wide the prudent savers are called upon to bail out reckless borrowers. Most savers receive close to zero percent interest on their savings, while they watch the price of food, petrol, and rents go up. Standards of living are falling for people depending on their savings while banks are bailed out and continue paying large bonuses.

The economy as a whole would contract dramatically if everyone spent less in order to pay down debts which would lead to recessions and depressions. The only way to make debt go away is through inflation as it wipes debt out over time. Inflation is just what the doctor would order for an economy with too much debt. While inflation is the friend of debtors it is the enemy of savers.

Most people are preparing for a repeat of a U.S style depression (deflation). These people feel secure hanging on to cash in savings, receiving a steady retirement check, reducing debt, cutting back on living expenses, and living a more simple life.

Although these people are well prepared for a U.S –style depression, they will be wiped out if we have a German-style depression (hyperinflation). Many mutual fund managers feel smart today because they got out of the market early and are now flush with cash. But what happens if a German-style depression is on the horizon? Will cash still be king? Will they still be smart?

At the moment the Fed is happy for asset values are propped up while the banks seem to get better and no one seems to notice while they are printing money on an unprecedented scale. Even if inflation slightly affects consumer prices, it can show up in asset prices leading to bubbles in stocks, commodities, land and other hard assets. But there is a very real danger that the Fed's money creating could suddenly turned into hyperinflation.

The effects of the Fed's policy are already appearing around the globe; higher inflation in China, higher food prices in Egypt and stock bubbles in Brazil.

Inflation would be more appealing in the beginning because assets prices would increase and diminish the weight of debt underlying those assets. People on fixed incomes will suffer as they will be unable to cope with the rising cost, as they have no chance of increasing their income so their lifestyle can only go down. As inflation gets higher more people will lose their jobs and the unemployment would increase, causing further reduction in spending until it threaten the very fabric of our society.

Things You Should Know

A few people are preparing for a deflation. These people are accumulating gold and silver coins, cash, and investments that adjust for inflation such as oil, food, gold and silver. Gold tends to rise along with inflation.

High inflation destroys personal wealth far more effectively than even deflation. High inflation destroys the value of all investments- cash included —making it much harder to preserve, let alone grow wealth. Energy would be expensive and the price of all consumer goods will skyrocket. Only a handful of independent thinkers would recognise where the real opportunities are and capitalise on it.

Deflation can destroy an economy, but individuals can preserve their wealth by trading in their investments for cash. During deflation prices fall, making cash worth more. You can actually increase the buying power of your savings by converting your assets into cash until the deflationary period has ended.

What to do/not to do in hyper-inflation.

(i) Cash, savings and short term deposits becomes the worst form of savings
(ii) Don't buy bonds because as the yields on bonds go up, the price goes down and vice versa.

(iii) Overall stock market prices will go down
(iv) Stock pile enough non-perishable food beforehand
(v) Buy gold bullion
(vi) Buy real estate
(vii) Buy shares in wind energy

What to do in a deflation

(i) Ensure you have enough cash. Cash and cash flow are critical to surviving the shakeout and having the resources to take advantage of unprecedented bargaining in financial assets in the years ahead.
(ii) Stock pile enough non-perishable food before hand
(iii) Get rid of your debt as much as possible
(iv) Be lean and mean in danger periods.
(v) Defer major capital expenditures.

Normal inflation

Inflation is very bad for people on fixed incomes; people who have no prospects of income growth such as retirees and their wealth would thus decrease as inflation increases.

To combat inflation you should invest in growth investments such as property which shows both capital and income growth over long periods of time.

Things You Should Know

Business types that do well during times of inflation are; aluminium, containers (metal and glass), gold and precious metals, natural gas, oil, food, and tobacco.

Business types that do poorly during times of inflation are; airlines, automobiles, computers, electric companies, furniture, and trucking companies.

The twelve benefits of a deflation crisis:

(i) Housing prices, the greatest single cost of living will come down.
(ii) Commercial real estate cost will fall lowering costs for business.
(iii) Massive amounts of private debt will be restructured.
(iv) The toughest will survive. The survival —of-the-fittest struggle in businesses will shift market share to the strongest businesses to give them greater scale and lower costs.
(v) Long-term entitlements will be restructured. The shift will reflect the reality of our longer life span.
(vi) Commodity prices will fall.
(vii) Dictatorships, too, will fall in emerging countries.
(viii) Developed countries will be more eco-conscious.
(ix) Restraints on global trade and immigration will diminish.

(x) Developed countries will trend into higher-value customized products and services.
(xi) Income inequality will decrease.
(xii) New technologies will be a driver.

33. The Global Currency Reset

Monetary rivalry is a fact of life in the world economy as it is the heart of global dominance. It was suggested that money is in essence the form of power. The relationship between currency and power however, is more complex than conventional wisdom would have us believe.

From the days of earliest coins, intense competition amongst currencies forced people to select a favourite currency for a period of time. The reason for this is that a single currency reduces trading cost and improves efficiency between countries.

Silver drachma, gold solidus, florin, ducat guilder, silver pesos, Deutsch mark, yen, pound sterling, the US dollar and the euro are all examples of these preferred currencies over time. It is costly to switch from one preferred currency to another. Switching to the next preferred currency as happened in the past proves beyond a doubt that no currency has ever enjoyed a permanent dominance for international use.

To be used as a preferable currency both economic and political factors are involved. On the economic side, demand is mostly shaped by the following three attributes.

First people must have widespread confidence in the particular currency's future value. The currency obtains this by having a proven track record of relatively low inflation and inflation variability.

Second are the qualities of exchange convenience and capital certainty. The currency must have the ability to sustain relatively large market orders without impacting on an individual asset price. The trading volumes and market competition must also ensure that the range between asking and selling prices are small and the market prices should recover quickly from un-usually large orders.

Finally, the currency must promise a broad transactional network. The greater the issuer's weight in global commerce, the stronger will be the attractiveness of its currency.

On the political side security, domestic and international considerations play a role. Domestically, political stability and effective governance play a role as backed by adequate protection of property rights, respect for the law and the enforcement of contractual obligations.

On the internationally side, foreign policies and strong defence capabilities are important.

The yen

At the end of World War II Japan lay in ruin, its economy shattered and its currency virtually worthless. Japan enjoyed an economic miracle, sustaining growth rates from thev1950s on ward that were the envy of the world. By 1960s Japan's GDP had come to be the second largest anywhere. By the late1970s, the international standing of the yen was well established. Just behind the US dollar. Yet Japan's currency too ultimately reached its limit and recently even gone in decline.

The yuan

China has emerged as an industrial and trading dynamo therefore many scholars believe that China's growing size and economic dominance will translate into their currency dominance. Few doubt that the country will have a major impact on the international monetary order in the years ahead. Despite the remarkable changes in China over the last three decades it remains far removed from standard Western models as the government maintains central control over a partly liberalised economy. The Communist Party has every reason to fear a loss of authority should its reins on the economy be loosened.

The Chinese government is trying their best to influence a wider foreign use of their currency to enhance their influence and prestige. To their dismay they are discovering that trust and credit do not solely depend on excellent GDP figures.

China however, is not ready to liberalise its domestic financial markets and to legalise capital inflows. They believe in a range of restrictions on more speculative market sectors to sustain their financial control. They are also afraid

Central banks would need to be given freedom to establish yuan bank accounts and to buy and sell selected classes of Chinese bonds and stocks. Potential investors are discouraged by the strict restraints over what they can do with their money.

The euro

When the euro was introduced in 1999 some economists predicted that the euro will challenge the status of the dollar and alter the power configuration of the system. The mainstream concurred that the US dollar would face a potent rival. Euro enthusiasm was by no means unjustified as the new currency credentials were excellent. The euro took off with a bang. Polls taken in 2008 indicated that the majority of Europeans expected their money to overtake the dollar within as little as five years.

Then the great crisis struck the world economy in 2008 just when Europeans were preparing to celebrate their currency's first decade. It showed that the EMU was flawed from the start because the European economy is diluted and their financial institutions are unable to match the liquidity and safety of the global dollar market. There is no clear delegation of authority within the EMU among national governments and their institutions. This makes the euro a currency without a country, its members a club of sovereign states. It is a product of a multi-state agreement with a fundamental mismatch between the domain of the euro zone and the legal jurisdictions of its participating governments. It was never stipulated who is in charge of the formulation, implementation, and the enforcement of rules of behaviour.

The euro critics said it is an experiment that failed, a broken marriage that requires a break up. For the euro supporters the implication is the reverse- that EMU will learn from its mistakes and become ever stronger. The reality is somewhere in between.

The US dollar

For decades America has been living beyond its means, relying too heavily on its undoubted power to delay. After decades of dollar supremacy the United States has come to take its exorbitant privilege for granted. The fault lies with the US policy makers, who have exploited the borrowing capacity afforded by the greenback's worldwide acceptability to postpone adjustments indefinitely. Republicans and Democrats find it difficult to agree even on something as simple as the weather, let alone how to reform the budget or manage the balance of payments. Jacob Frenkel, former head of the Bank of Israel said in 2005, "I am concerned with the US current-account deficit, not because it cannot be dealt with but because of the way it is not being dealt with." More than a decade later the risk is still not being dealt with.

Since the Global Financial Crisis of 2007-08, there have been numerous calls from countries such as Russia and China to abandon the U.S.$. as the single major reserve currency and bring in a new reserve currency or currencies.

The BRICS countries signed an agreement in 2012 to trade in their own currencies and no longer use the U.S.$ for trade. The following year they funded their developing bank to finance infrastructure and development projects amongst them. The BRICS nations are also buying up many tonnes of gold.

The proposed change is also likely to initiate the Global Currency Reset (GCR) whereby all currencies are to be re-valued or devalued depending on the assets of the country and the strength of the economy.

This is also in line with the Wall Street bankers to devise an international monetary system that more consistently aligns the interest of individual countries with the interest of the global economy as a whole. In particular such a system would provide more effective checks on the tendency for countries to run large and persistent external imbalances, whether surpluses or deficits. The U.S.$ will lose its reserve status and the petrodollar will cease to exist.

The problem is that neither the Euro nor the Yuan can take over from the U.S.$ on short notice. Therefore, the countries would have to return to the gold standard in the interim until enough of the new currency could be printed and distributed.

The price of gold would be fixed for central banks and gold would be used as an asset for trade between central banks. The great advantage is that gold is nobody's liability and it can't be printed.

The GCR would not be a smooth

transition, for the change- over will be preceded by a global economic crisis. This would be a much greater crisis than the 2007-08 crisis. The global economy which is built on cheap money is going to topple when interest rates are raised which would crash the stock and derivatives markets.

This would lead to massive bankruptcies, bank failures, pension confiscations, and a one off tax on private wealth to restore debt sustainability. It's not going to be a pleasant world.

Once this huge credit bubble has burst it would be too late for the people to do anything. When the people realise the banks have closed their doors and they cannot withdraw their money they would panic but it would be too late. The alternative is they will wake up one morning to find that prices have doubled, while their bank balances have been reduced.

34. Machine Intelligence

Many of us have striven to work at something that is not only well paid but is meaningful and important. We want to contribute something substantial.

André Klopper

The truth is that a lot of young people are facing diminishing job opportunities, even several years after the formal end of the recession in 2009, when the economy began to once again expand after a historic contraction. The youth who lack the right training mean they are being shut out of opportunities like never before. Being young and having no proper job remains stubbornly common.

It was true in the great Industrial Revolution of the nineteenth century and it is true now: machines do not put us all out of work as eventually machines create new jobs just as they destroy old ones. It is also true that new machines of our age will give rise to new and different workplaces and create a new set of winners and losers.

The wave of the increasing ability of machines to substitute intelligent human labour will lift you or dump you. Workers will be classified more and more into two categories. The key question will be; are you good at working with intelligent machines or not? If you and your skills are complementary to the computer your wage and labour market prospects are rosy. If your skills do not complement the computer, you may want to address that mismatch.

The concept of standardisation is already in the workplace and most of us use information to judge possible career paths or to advise others.

Things You Should Know

It is a reality that in America more than 60 percent of U.S employers check credit scores on potential employees before hiring. This is scary when standardisation is applied to social and economic relations as a whole.

Machines aren't just about producing goods and services at lower cost; they also will improve the quality of service in the professions. Sooner or later most professionals, especially at the top end of the market will be graded by a team of skilled workers cooperating with smart machines.

The lessons learned about labour and machines up to now are:

1. Human-computer teams are the best teams

2. The person working the smart machine doesn't have to be an expert in task at hand.

3. Below some critical level of skill, adding a man to the machine will make the team less effective than the machine working alone.

4. Knowing one's own limits is more important than it used to be.

Science is a general framework for making predictions, controlling our environment, and understanding our world. As science progresses, each new marginal discovery is more the result of specialisation and less the result of general breakthroughs, compared to earlier times.

The practice and understanding of science is in for some major changes due to mechanical intelligence. We are at the crux of a technological revolution once again. The computer will become more central to the actual research, even to the design of the research program, and the human will become the handmaiden rather than the driver of progress.

Science will become harder to understand for the following reasons:

1. In some scientific areas problems are becoming more complex and unsusceptible to simple intuitive, big breakthroughs.

2. The individual scientific contribution is becoming more specialised, a trend that has been running for centuries and is unlikely to stop.
3. One day soon, intelligent machines will become formidable researchers in their own right.

Although most scientists predict that mechanical intelligence will gradually change the world; there are those that disagree. Eliezer Yudkowsky, the well-known futurist and speculative thinker offers a bleak prediction. We wake up one day and find that a super-intelligent machine has taken over the world.

Eliezer fears a cascade. Once a very good

program becomes sufficiently developed it will create other programs, which in turn will create other capabilities. The combined ability of all these programs could explode exponentially and, supposedly, have a lot of power.

If we're talking about the distant future, we must assume virtually anything is possible. The evidence so far however doesn't suggest this kind of unstable cascade to be very likely. Even the strongest programs need human assistance every step of the way.

35. Disposition towards Money

Optimistic people believe yesterday was good, today is good why should tomorrow be any different. The catastrophe they read about in the newspapers, or see on TV happens to other people.

Few people realise that the root of our problem is our money-the very thing they work and hang on to. It is the lies we believe about what money can do for us and the dumb decisions we make out of ignorance that causes so much misery.

What we have established thus far in this book is there is not only a flaw in the prevailing economic model but also flaws in our society. Too many people had taken advantage of others. A sense of trust had been broken Almost every day has brought stories of bad behaviour by those in the financial sector-Ponzi schemes, insider trading, predatory lending, and a host of credit card schemes to extract as much from the hapless user as possible.

We are part of a society in which materialism dominates moral commitment, in which the rapid growth that we have achieved is not sustainable environmentally or socially, in which we do not act together as a community to address our common needs.

If you ask people how much money they want you usually get the following five common answers.

1. More money than I have now.

2. As much money as I can get.

3. Enough money that I'll never have to worry again.

4. More money than I could ever possibly need.

5. More money than my neighbour/brother/parents/boss/enemy has or will ever have.

Besides lacking specificity, these non-answers have in common is that; they aren't

Things You Should Know

there yet and they want more..

Many people want to be millionaires for they want to experience what they believe only millions can buy. Many millionaires are unhappy by spending time with people they don't like and buying things they don't need and measuring their success in the number of their trophy wives. The lesson is that life is all about compromise-none of us can have absolutely everything we want,

Have you ever wondered why one person can just manage fine on $36,000 a year, while another person is in big trouble on $360,000? The first person is not living like a hermit and the second person does not gamble. The difference between the two individuals is mainly due to their disposition towards money.

Millions of people remain stuck in the same financial predicament even though they've tried everything they know to get ahead. They suspect that there has to be a better way to make lasting, profound changes in their financial life that they crave for. But still 67% of all adults couldn't tell you within 10% of what they spend in an average month.

To drive a car on the roads you have to learn how to drive and you have to pass a test to prove you know the laws and rules. You also have to pass a road test to prove you are a safe, knowledgeable driver.

André Klopper

Managing your income skilfully is at least as important as your ability to drive a car. Although the total amount of money that will flow through your hands and which you will control during your lifetime is significant, the chances are high that you entered your adult life without any financial training.

Sadly, most people entered adulthood lacking personal financial intelligence. They have no rules to follow, not even a list of suggestions or any kind of mental framework for how to manage an income or even what that would look like.

You have to learn the rules nobody told you and nobody talks about, and you have to learn fast. Open your mind to a new perspective about money and explore new possibilities. The reason why so many "how to get rich" books fail to deliver is that the authors only explain one set of rules assuming everyone is exactly the same.

If I make a statement that most people don't treat all their money the same quite a number of readers would object to that statement. However, if a person were to receive $200 in back salary they will most properly treat it different than the $200 in their bank account or the $200 they won in a shopping spree. For most people the easier they obtained the money the easier they would spend it.

Most people would think hard before

spending $400 on a new car radio but will not hesitate to pay $400 extra for a car radio when purchasing a $16,000 car. Exactly the same amount for the same thing but in different circumstances. The same principle applies when people buy insurance with their flat screen TV without blinking an eye but will not buy insurance a month after they had bought the TV.

The message of the book is not about how to get rich but it is worthwhile to know why some people struggle with money and became money's slaves while others prosper and became money's masters. It does not provide a quick fix but it does provide a better understanding of who we really are, why we behave in certain ways, and what the root causes of our suffering are. Making money is not a reason for being in business. It is a by-product.

In order to simplify things I would categorise people into six main groups, the poor, the over-spenders, the conservative, the in between people, the risk takers and the controllers. The in between people are those that fit in more than one category, depicting them as progressing into the next stage or finding themselves comfortable in-between.

The poor people-

These are the poor people with the ability to control their own finances and not the poor people living in poor countries. The poor people are those having little money. Their focus is on scarcity. A lot of them struggle just to feed their families from day to day, through no fault of their own. They feel shame and embarrassment regarding financial matters. They think of money as; the root of all evil, in the way of their happiness, and it corrupts.

As they are not self-sufficient they usually experience a fair amount of guilt and a great deal of insecurity, even though most keep it well hidden. In today's world, money is synonymous with survival, and everybody wants to survive.

The poor believe the rich don't see the extent of their own privilege, and if the rich share their wealth more equally the suffering would diminish. If you are in this category you need to work hard on your financial mindset and get educated in financial matters.

Observing poverty one person once asked another, "Why- given all the suffering and inequality in the world-didn't we just redistribute all the wealth so that everybody could have equal portions. That seemed a fair thing."

The other person responded by saying," before too long, it would end up right back where it started."

The best welfare program is a job.

The over-spenders:

The over-spenders are people who use money to impress other people as they crave for attention, recognition, respect and prestige. It is very important for them to have the best things in their neighbourhood for their neighbours to observe success.

They go into debt in order to look rich. It is hip to sport the latest designer handbag, use the latest technology in phones and computers while driving expensive cars and belong to an exclusive club.

They receive many praises for their appearance confirming their belief, 'clothes make the man'. It is from others they gain their own sense of identity.

They usually don't have a budget and therefore struggle to pay their accounts if something goes wrong. They believe they don't have the time or the expertise to develop a sound financial plan. They even fail to apply simple guidelines which can help them avoid financial troubles or disaster. Some even try to borrow regularly from their rich friends and relatives but struggle to repay them.

Their predominant message is that it's all about money; that more money or a different set of financial circumstances will bring them the freedom to stop worrying and just enjoy life.

Disadvantages for some over-spenders:

(i) Constantly fighting over the other's extravagant shopping sprees.

(ii) Their primary pleasure is when buying something they want, their wanting to stop for the moment. But soon after they want something else or better.

(iii) They focus on objects and experiences as their source of happiness.

(iv) They believe money is to be used to enjoy life.

(v) Their debt exceeds their assets.

The conservatives-

The conservatives do what they have been taught to do; they go to school, work hard, pay their bills, save, invest their money in mutual funds and prepare for their future. They have a budget and are in control of their money and would now and again reward themselves for their money discipline by buying something they really want.

They believe financial insecurities are mainly the result of the choices people make, not the income they earn. Therefore, if you do not take charge of your finances, they will take charge of you. Yogi Berra said "You've got to be very careful if you don't know where you are going, you might not get there." In other words they firmly believe they need a plan. They live below their means but calculate their net worth after they have been in contact with the over-spenders.

They also believe there is more to a good life than making money. When it comes to happiness, non-financial assets such as a good marriage, family, friends, self-fulfilling work, religious beliefs, and enjoyable hobbies are far more important than money.

<u>Disadvantages for some conservatives:</u>

(i) Investing; for some of them the timing is never right, the conditions are never perfect so they put it off to quit their job, make that important decision or invest in their dreams. "Someday" is a disease that will take their dreams to the grave with them.

(ii) Frugal to the point of deprivation, and not enjoying life as they constantly feel guilty if they had spent money.

(iii) Savers are almost always afraid that their money might run out one day and leave them poor, alone, or dependent on others.

(iv) Focusing on fear will make your strategies more defensive.

The risk takers-

These are the people that take calculated risks, who think outside the square and don't believe everything they were taught. Risk takers are not gamblers but know that greater risks and higher returns go together. The successful ones are always very knowledgeable about their business, competitors, technology and their environment. Their focus is on abundance.

They believe;

a) Life doesn't have to be so damn hard.

b) To have others work for you.

c) To be neither the boss nor the employee, but the owner.

d) To have more quality and less clutter.

e) To think big, but ensure payday comes every day: cash flow first, big payday second.

f) Not to have all things they want to have, but to do all the things they want to do, and be all the things they want to be.

g) To challenge the Status Quo

h) A high savings rate often adds to their wealth.

i) They emphasize their strengths and don't fix their weaknesses

j) Money alone is not the solution

k) They are not afraid of failing; they just keep on trying until they succeed

<u>What they must be aware of:</u>

(i) Not ever happy with their net worth

(ii) Too focused on increasing their wealth that they trod on everyone else

(iii) Owning a business is risky, many small businesses fail.

<u>The controllers-</u>

They are a very small minority of less than 1% of the population who owns more than 80% of the earth's wealth. They can never have enough although they get a great thrill from achieving their grand and impressive goals therefore they spend a disproportionate amount of time focusing on the future.

They know by controlling the money supply they control us. They want us to need more and more of their toxic money. The more we need money, the more money they can print.

The more the populace need money, the weaker we become and the easier for them to control us. In their aim for material gain to control the world they have caused many wars, destruction and misery.

I had read an article in a property magazine about a rich Australian property investor giving lectures on how to become rich with properties. After one of his lectures one of the guests complimented him on how it was the most inspiring speech that he had listened to during the last ten years. The investor then asked him how many investment properties the guest owns. The guest replied none for he had not yet found the right time to buy.

The investor wrote in the magazine that is no use in attending lectures about how to get rich with properties, if you don't go out and buy the investment properties. Walk the talk he wrote. He explained that if the guest had bought a house just after attending his first seminar he would have made a handsome profit for the average house price in Sydney had doubled over the last ten years. He is right of course but first you have to change your disposition towards money before you can invest in properties. He also assumed the guest had thousands of dollars lying around, just waiting for the right investment.

Change your disposition-

Although it would be difficult, people can change their disposition towards money if they so wish. Here are some basic questions to prompt you in changing your behaviour;

a) Define your nightmare, the absolute worst that could happen if you did what you are considering. Envision them in painstaking detail and determine how likely it is that it would actually happen.

b) What steps could you take to prevent or minimise the damage if something does go wrong.

c) What are the temporary and permanent outcomes?

d) If you are fired from your job today, what would you do to get things under financial control?

e) What are you putting off out of fear? It is fear of unknown outcomes that prevent you from doing what you need to do.

f) What is it costing you-financially, emotionally, and physically-to postpone action? If you don't pursue those things that excite you, where will you be in one year, five years, and ten years? If the answer is one of disappointment and regret then inaction is the greatest risk of all.

g) What are you waiting for? The answer is simple you're afraid just like the rest of the world.

'I went to the bank and reviewed my savings. I found out I have all the money I'll ever need. If I die tomorrow.' - Henny Youngman

36. Important Things

The most important things that can really make or break your happiness are: how much contact you have with good friends and company; simple good fun, whether or not you have a satisfying relationship with a partner or spouse, and whether or not you get real job satisfaction from your work.

Our deeper psychological needs are for love, a feeling of power or self-worth, belonging, freedom to choose and fun. Money can buy none of the above but good friendships with the people around us will steer us in the right direction.

"If you have health, you probably will be happy, and if you have health and happiness, you have all the wealth you need, even if it is not all you want." - Elbert Hubbard.

Choosing contentment as a way of life is the only way to win the battle between needs vs. wants. Contentment is choosing to be happy with what you have, while not always desiring something more.

Contentment is not something we achieve; it is a choice we make. It is an attitude we learn. It's a decision we make to buy what we need and want what we have.

Prosperity does not bring contentment, and poverty cannot take it away. Read that again. Contentment is that settled place where we are at peace knowing that while we may not have it all, we do have enough. We have enough for survival, enough for comfort, and enough to meet our needs.

<u>Living well on less</u>

a) With determination you can be happy while spending less.

b) Keep away from shopping malls.

c) Best things in life are free.

d) Don't enter the supermarket on an empty stomach.

e) Only buy the items on your shopping list and which are in season.

f) Shop smart-not what you like but what you need.

g) Eating from your own garden all year round.

h) Learn by asking for advice or by reading.

You need to spend money to lose money. This is very true when you spend money on something that eventually becomes worthless. We buy a lot of items that we rarely or never use. In most cases, the goal shouldn't be to find a way to use it; the goal should be to find a way not to buy it in the first place. After all, if we own something but never use it, certainly our quality of life will not suffer if we avoid the purchase altogether. Remember there's nothing wrong with admitting you can't handle money.

A balanced lifestyle

A preacher once gave his members this sound advice; "earn as much as you can, save as much as you can, and give to others as much as you can."

A balanced lifestyle is the right amount of this, the right amount of that and not too much of any one thing-and you have the formula for a sustainable, lifetime plan. When your money is in balance, you spend just the right amount on each of your three basic expense categories. The three basic categories are;

1) Your Must Haves (the things you need)

2) Your Savings (the money you save and for helping others)

3. Your wants (the stuff that is just for fun)

When you get your money into balance, your money worries fade away.

Live within your means and stay there. This is about avoiding one of the greatest modern-day financial pitfalls: allowing your expenses to rise to meet or even exceed your income. It's about establishing a permanent standard of living, one that's both comfortable and affordable, rather than constantly chasing an escalating standard of living. It's about not becoming dependent on a salary and lifestyle that might be unsustainable or, in the end, unsatisfying. Once you've settled on what's enough for you, can stop thinking about it and get on with enjoying life.

Seven money rules-

1. Spend less than you earn.

It is the only way you will experience financial

freedom. It is something you make happen. It is a decision. It is the attitude you choose for how you will conduct your life and manage your money. Remember that consumer credit generally motivates you to spend more than what you earn and to build wealth you must spend less than what you earn. You work hard for your money and you have to work harder at keeping it.

2. Save for the future

The antidote for financial fear is money in the bank. It changes everything because you lose that broke feeling. Money in the bank changes your outlook because it changes your attitude. As your savings grow, so do your options, and with options come hope for the future. Saving money strategically and with purpose does more than accumulate money, it develops character traits of self-reliance and financial maturity.

Money will work for you if you put it to work, and the longer it works for you, the more wealth you will build.

3. Give some away

Greed will do all it can to make sure we will never find contentment. It is selfish creating a desire to have more and more and is never good.

Greed is like a cancer that when left untreated can destroy individuals, families, businesses, governments and economies.

Breaking the stronghold of greed by giving develops the following;

a) Develops personal compassion. Putting other's needs ahead of your own selfish desires.

b) Develops generosity. A heart filled with gratitude expresses itself with generosity. Generosity kills greed.

c) Put other's needs ahead of your wants.

d) By regularly giving money and time away you are growing into a more meaningful person.

4. Anticipate your irregular expenses. Many people don't budget for irregular expenses and are caught out when something major breaks down and have to be repaired or replaced.

.

5. Tell your money where to go. A budget is the ticket to financial happiness and has to be written down. Divide it into income, essential fixed expenses, essential variable expenses, non-essential expenses, miscellaneous expenses, and the total. Then track your spending and determine where you can save.

People who don't have a budget think it is boring, a hassle and time consuming. These problems can be solved with a few simple tools, many of which you'll find online.

6. Manage your credit. Beware having a credit card without financial knowledge or self-control may put you at risk. Don't buy more with your card than what you can easily pay in full at the end of that month. If you can't clear your card each and every month then stop using your card.

7. Borrow only what you know you can repay. Debt is not ideal but tolerated in certain situations and only for a defined period of time under rigid guidelines. You have to use caution as it limits your options and it is expensive. All debts fall into one of three categories:

- o Reasonable; buying something that has a high likelihood of increasing in value.
- o Toxic: toxic debt is hazardous to your wealth and are credit card debt, payday loans, or from money lenders.
- o Neutral debt includes all other borrowing that is neither good nor bad.

Spending decisions-

Things You Should Know

Before spending any money first go through the following questions. It will take a moment and help you to focus on what you are about to do. It offers you time to think and in most cases your desire will dissipate.

1 Do you really need this?
2. Do you have something already that will do just as well?
3. Are you sure it is a good value?
4. Do you have cash to pay for it?
5. Could you delay the purchase for a few weeks or months?
6) Are you willing to delay your decision for 24 hours before acting?

Make a "What was I thinking?" list and carry it with you at all times. Fold it into business card size to fit neatly into your wallet to make a list of purchases that you regret. Next time you get ready to make a discretionary purchase, take a few moments to read "What was I thinking?" list, and maybe you'll decide to pass.

37. Changing Course

This is a critical wake-up call, challenging everyone to act. Since the Great Recession of 2007/8 millions are unemployed, others are struggling with huge debt all the while the U.S. dollar is heading into a downward spiral. All major economies have merely kicked the can further down the road and we all know that if you ignore problems, they get bigger.

You feel there is absolutely nothing you can do about it anyway. You are absolutely right, therefore stop dwelling on what you can't change and focus on the things you do control, your personal economy. Hope for the best and plan for the worst.

Consider cooperatives. When Argentina went into an economic crisis in 2001 a quarter of the population was unemployed; middle class disappeared into the poor working class. People went hungry and turned desperate, leading to a surge in violence and crime.

At one point people began working on their own, fixing the machines in the bankrupted factories and began manufacturing things again. Through democratic procedures, the workers decided how they would spend the profits, first paying off the debts the factory owed to get it back on its feet, then spreading the rest out in salary among themselves.

Since then the cooperative model has flourished, and Argentina is again a thriving economy less than a decade after the crash. Today there are 16,000 cooperatives in Argentina, employing 300,000 people and making up 10 percent of the nation's GDP.

Things You Should Know

Any kind of change should be approached as a challenge that calls for endurance and a survivor's spirit, it is hard work. It is hard to make changes because they are so ingrained. Breaking the habits of a lifetime is never going to be easy as you have to change course in flight.

Knowledge is a wonderful thing but until you put those things you have learned into action it is nothing more than entertainment. Therefore, having a clear vision of what you want to achieve and knowing what you don't want is meaningless unless you act on it. Stop saying that I will do it someday and instead ask yourself why not today?

Economic hardship affects not only your financial well-being; it will also take a toll on your physical and emotional well-being. If you are not in control of your finances, the things you worry about become a source of chronic stress.

The journey into new territory might be frightening but if you don't change you will surely regret it. Regret is a good thing but it ALWAYS comes too late. There are things which stop us from reaching our dreams but most of them are ease to fix once we set our mind to it.

If the task seems too daunting break it down into small steps and take one small step at a time. Even the longest journey starts with the first step.

Steps and ways to make the transition easier-

Step 1: Know what you're trying to accomplish. Do your homework.

Step 2: Change your attitude. Nothing will happen unless you want it to happen. It starts in your head and it is the plain and practical truth. Resist adapting an "all or nothing" mentality and go for, "I will do the best I can".

Step 3: Believe that it is possible. If you keep on telling yourself I can't do this then of course you can't do it. But if you believe you can then you will do it.

Unless you BELIEVE success is possible, NOTHING will change. Get rid of negative thoughts. Living with doubt and fear can become a habit and after a while you begin to believe there is no other way.

Ban the following three words, Never, Always and Forever out of your vocabulary and replace them with I WILL DO MY BEST.

It is too hard; is just an excuse for not willing to put in some effort and stick with it.

Putting the blame on others; convincing yourself that you're off the hook. There is always someone you can blame and the reasons will always be good but are downright destructive. Focus on yourself and what you plan to do about it.

Waiting for the right time, situation, or circumstances? It is just another excuse not to act but to procrastinate.

Make sure everyone in your family is on board.

Step 4: Set a clear goal in what you want to achieve and the time lines of when you want to achieve your goal. Even if your goal seems unattainable at first glance, it still serves as a great source of inspiration. If you aim for the stars, you may at least hit the moon. Goal setting is absolutely essential if you want to make progress. Your objective must be attainable steps towards your goal. How do you walk five hundred miles? One step after another until you reaches your destination. How do you move a mountain? One wheelbarrow at a time until the task is completed.

You must realise that nothing comes from nothing.

Step 5: Set aside the time to do it right, both initially and ongoing.

Get help where you need it

Step 6: Have a plan for the transition; know where you're going and how to get there. Failing to plan is planning to fail. Plan, and plan early, for planning reduces fear of the future and fear of failure. Even a few ideas with some numbers written on a sheet of paper will help defeat the insecurities that you may have. Setting specific, actionable, motivating goals will turbo charge your efforts.

Step 7: Make the commitment. If you are serious about it, say it aloud, discuss it with your family and write it down. By writing down your goal it makes it more likely that you will achieve it. This is one of the most important commitments you may ever make, so take it seriously. Picture your goal, look, think, focus and act on it every day. Remember we are what we think.

Step 8: Always aspire to something meaningful. Therefore don't waste time on something insignificant. Few people would deny that there is a lot of desperate need in the world and that money can help to alleviate human suffering. Kindness is needed where welfare systems look poised to sink. Kindness form part of a personal finance plan because giving is good and has been identified as one of the top five actions that increase happiness and well-being. Don't just believe what you read or what you're told, experiment yourself to test the legitimacy of the lesson.

Step 9: Keep your emotions in check.

a) Identify where you're vulnerable and take steps to protect yourself.

b) Protect yourself from temptation and keep away from those things that stop you from reaching your goal.

c) Alone: get support and the simple act of describing your struggles can help put them into perspective.

d) If at first you don't succeed try and try again. See failure as a necessary part of learning.

Step 10: Study your progress, analyse and review your choices; drop the ones that aren't adding much; try others for size. Realise it is natural for our goals to change over time.

<u>Things stopping us from reaching our potential-</u>

1) Fear of change and fear of what others might think.

2) Feelings of insecurity.

3) No goal setting: no timelines, no defined goals, nothing written down.

4) The excessive worries about things that may or may not happen.

5) Emotions:

What crises should have taught us is that bad stuff does happen and that a careful, well-thought out diversified strategy is essential.

The ultimate goal is financial freedom, a position where your money and time are your own. Your physical, mental and emotional well-being may not feature on a budget spreadsheet, but in many ways they should.

Work less-

Reduced hours, the ability to keep earning and stay actively engaged in society, while continuing to be usefully and gainfully employed for longer.

Steps to get out of poverty-

a) Change your mindset towards money.

b) Read and learn about finances.

c) Change your spending behaviour.

d) Set goals.

e) Implement a budget

Things You Should Know

A budget is simply a way of organising your spending so that you can live within your means and achieve your goals. It's a tool, not a punishment for the sins of overspending.

The less money you have, the more you need to be able to account for every single dollar you have spent. With a budget you decide how to allocate your monthly income to your monthly expenses, what those expenses will be, and how much you will save each month. A budget is the first step towards getting control of your finances and increasing your net worth.

Tips to change our disposition towards money-

Passion and skills:

a) Discover where your passion lies. Enjoy what you do, and believe it is important, for you will do more of it and work harder to do it better.

b) You will achieve higher income levels when you specialize in those things you do best.

c) You are usually better off if you are good at something that is highly valued by others.

Money:

a) Knowledge about financial matters is important.

b) Learn to control cash flow.

c) You must be proud to be frugal and spend money more wisely.

d) You make yourself better off by increasing your opportunities, not by reducing them.

e) Financial success is about making your services more valuable than others.

Opportunities:

a) Prepare for the unexpected

b) Do something exciting and challenging EVERYDAY.

c) Discover better ways of doing things

Steps to improve your finances:

a) Change your personal spending behaviour.

   - Un-clutter your life from things you don't need.

   - Make every dollar you spend count.

- Reduce the hold that money has over your life.

- Don't use excuses like it is only $10.

- Hope is not a plan.

- Pay your bills on time.

- Consider moving to a cheaper area of the country.

b) Set goals, incentives matter, so put them to work for you.

c) Devise a plan of action; create a personal budget with actual and proposed goals.

d) Take the plunge; do it.

e) Don't finance anything for longer than its useful life.

f) Get more out of your money; avoid credit cards and consider buying used items.

g) Let compound interest work for you.

Pitfalls to avoid-

Goals:

a) Losing sight of your dreams.

b) Viewing one product, job, or project as the end-all and be-all of your existence.

c) Blowing small problems out of proportion.

d) Don't view your home as a reliable investment that will fund your retirement.

Wasting precious time:

a) Micromanaging and e-mailing to fill the time.

b) Handling problems someone else is paid to do.

c) Helping people with the same problem over and over.

d) Chasing non-profitable customers.

e) Answering e-mails which will not lead to a sale.

f) Answering e-mails which could be answered by a FAQ or auto-responder.

g) Striving for endless perfection.

h) Making non-time-sensitive issues urgent.

Risks:

a) Beware of investment schemes with high returns and little risk.

b) Deal only with parties that have a reputation to protect.

c) Do not allow yourself to be forced into a quick decision.

d) Do not allow friendships to influence an investment decision.

Rewards:

a) Do not ignore the social rewards of life.

b) Teach your children how to earn money and spend it wisely.

38. The Meltdown: Why, When, Where and Who

Yogi Berra once said: "Prediction is difficult, especially about the future."

Once you eliminate the impossible, whatever remains, no matter how improbable, must be the truth. Sherlock Holmes.

We can't see the future and in particular the macro future, but with all this uncertainty you have to understand the economic, political and social environment we live in.

Every country has a contingency plan for what to do in a case of war with its neighbours, none of the countries have a contingency plan for its citizens in the case of a financial meltdown.

People think they don't need a plan in a financial crisis because it is not going to happen, then they get punched in the face, and everything around them becomes foggy, then it is too late to plan.

The purpose of this chapter is not to scare or to depress you but to raise your awareness and help you get through the downward phase of the economic cycle. It is important to be conscious about what can go wrong when the market falls back, because that's when the pressure increases. The information in the following chapters is to help you weather the storm. If you follow the advice you might even prosper in the downturn.

I hope the information thus far has convinced you of the benefits of becoming a more open-minded and emotionally intelligent person.

I believe we are entering a long and hard financial winter. The good news is that spring will come, flowers will bloom, and a new life will be born. Eventually we will come out of this financial crisis, but unfortunately millions of people will be permanently left behind. For their sake I hope their governments will save them, or can save them.

<u>Reasons why a meltdown is inevitable-</u>

International:

1) The world governments did not solve the 2008 financial crisis, only delayed it

2) Britain's debt is more than 5 times its GDP and is worse than in Europe.

3) Japan the world's third largest economy is in deficit and has started a currency war.

4) BRICS countries are no longer trading in U.S.$ amongst themselves, placing pressure on the U.S. dollar

5) Countries are phasing out the petrodollar

6) In 2004 Greenspan said the rest of the world would not be willing to finance U.S. deficit forever

7) China is responsible for $3.6 trillion in loans annually

8) China will soon be the richest country and

are already asking why the dollar is the reserve currency of the world.

9) In the developed countries the asset prices are about to burst while unemployment is already high at high levels.

U.S. government-

1) For the last nine years the U.S. has been running at almost a zero % interest rate causing inflated real estate markets and a stock market bubble.

2) Printing fiat money with no back-up leading to a bubble in the bond market.

3) The annual deficit is more than $1 trillion and growing while the dollar is being devalued

4) Government deficit grew from $3.0 trillion in 1984 to $17.5 trillion and they can no longer afford to repay the interest.

5) U.S. debt slope of 10% before gold standard was dropped and 50% after Gold standard was dropped.

6) U.S. financial system is built on a giant Ponzi scheme.

7) Highways and bridges are in need of major repair.

8) In order to achieve GDP growth U.S. debt must rise to $166 trillion by 2023 and be paying back $26.5 trillion annually.

9) Major airlines such as Pan American are history, and giants such as United Airlines are on life support.

U.S citizens-

1) For the last 25 years the median income in the U.S. remained at $51,000

2) U.S. household debt rose from $13 trillion in 1989 to $58 trillion in 2012

3) Most U.S. rich people have moved out of the cities

4) U.S. inside traders have all sold most of their stock

5) The U.S suburbs struggle, major shopping centres face trouble and retailers close their doors while online shopping is taking off.

6) Baby boomers are retiring requiring pension and health care

7) Pension plans are going broke.
<u>Is the economic crisis just a hoax</u>?

1) Well not for the people living in Greece, Spain, Italy, and Detroit.

2) Not for the 1% of wealthy Americans who moved into the rural areas.

3) Not for the inside traders.

4) Did you know about the 2008 crises which is not resolved.

5) Did you lose sight of Lehman brothers, Freddie Mac and Fannie Mae?

6) A $1 quadrillion in derivatives trade.

7) The past 10 years credit growth was 12% per year and GDP growth 4% per year.

8) 47 million people in the U.S. are on food relief.

Things You Should Know

When will it happen?

The financial meltdown is like a missile that has already been launched, it is silently hurtling towards us. We are just waiting for the impact.

Will it be slowly phased in?

1) The answer is NO the dollar bubble will come on very quickly and will be too large for central banks to solve.

2) Most people would be blindsided

3) As most people live from pay check to pay check they will suffer

4) People are complacent and will not see it coming

5) Only 3 million out of 312 million in America are prepared.

What will happen?

Financial and travel

    1) Hike in interest rates.

    2) Wall Street in downward spiral until

shut down.

3) Banks would respond; closing their doors or restrict cash with-drawls.

4) U.S. dollar would lose its value.

5) U.S. would import less and other counties would scale down.

6) Assets including fine art, collectables and jewellery will fall to stunning lows.

7) Travel sector would be affected as people would travel less.

Jobs and businesses

1) Capital goods sector: the automotive, construction, industrial equipment will be very vulnerable and would suffer huge losses and many people in this industry would lose their jobs.

2) The discretionary spending sector: travel, tourism, restaurants, and entertainment sectors will fare better than the capital goods sector. However people would travel less and spend less as people experience the downturn.

Things You Should Know

3) The necessities sector: in the job market the necessities sector is the place to be as this sector will do better than the other two sectors.

4) Many small business would close down.

5) Workers in their millions would lose their jobs.

6) Fierce competition for fewer jobs will cause a reduction in wages.

7) A number of million people would lose their homes.

8) A shrinking middle class.

9) Just as some poorer people will do without fancy infrastructure, so will others do without advance healthcare. The world will look much more unfair and much less equal and indeed it will be.

André Klopper

Panic

    1) Life as we know it will cease to exist.

    2) People would lose their liquidity.

    3) People will be angry.

    4) People would only buy food and necessities.

    5) Desperate people would panic.

In the extreme scenario

    1) Pension funds would go bankrupt.

    2) Food stores would run out of food.

    3) Panic would spread.

    4) Riots and looting would take place all around the world.

    5) Marshal Law would be implemented.

    6) Millions would die especially children and the elderly.

Aftershock

1) Government debt bubble would be last to burst.

2) People would reject money and begin to barter.

3) Debt would be reset maybe with a new Eurodollar.

Which countries would suffer most?

1) Poor countries such as Africa would suffer the most as most foreign aid will come to a standstill. Foreign investments will dry up and countries would demand repayments on their loans. Sub-Saharan Africa about half the population is stuck in extreme poverty, a proposition that has hardly budged since 1981.

2) Developing countries such as India, Indonesia, South Africa, Mexico and Brazil would suffer quite severely as their exports would nose dive while foreign capital will dry up.

3) America would suffer the most of the developed countries as it is on the period of diminishing returns and for the short term

there is only one way and that is down.

4) Western Europe will suffer second least. The yen and euro will hold up relative to the dollar as Europe and China won't have massive outflow of capital as the U.S. This is only if Europe stays united.

5) Although China will suffer the least it will face the multiplier effect. For each job created to produce export sold to U.S. markets two more jobs are created to support these jobs. Most jobs would be suspended.

Both China and India need an annual growth of at least 8% just to provide jobs for the tens of millions joining the workforce each year. For China growth is essential.

This is the same for Korea, Taiwan, Hong Kong and Singapore.

China has a booming economy ready to burst in real estate, stock market, banking and construction industries

Who will suffer?

1) Foreign investors in U.S. will suffer tremendous losses.

2) Countries with huge government debt will be strapped for cash and thus forced to drastically reduce social welfare programs.

3) The number of middle class would be greatly reduced forcing them into poverty.

5 places not to be when it happens:

1) Africa
2) Israel
3) America
4) Britain
5) China
6) All major cities

39. What Should We Do?

Our only hope out of this mess is that our governments nationalise the Reserve Banks and provide new guidelines, redirecting them to operate the business for the benefit of the public. Also establish the Reserve Bank with its own economic sovereignty. By law the state must deposit all its funds in the bank, which pays a competitive rate of interest to the state treasurer. The bank has to provide the state's own credit, and issue its own currency.

Every country in the past who took control away from the bankers and operated the state bank for the benefit for their citizens has turned their economy around and prospered. If this don't happen we must prepare for the worst.

To survive the financial storms ahead you need to be vigilant, be able to perceive events from a different perspective, and have the knowledge and expertise to act upon perceived opportunities. Your knowledge, expertise and mindset will ultimately determine your success.

How we respond to everything around us in these changing times depends upon our purpose in life. What are the most important things in your life? Are you able to lead, manage, support and love those around you?

Each of us defines for ourselves what it means to be successful and being more successful means more of who you are capable of being. We also have to pay attention to what is really important.

We have to learn from the past, obtain something valuable from it so when the same situation arises we can do things differently, not making the same mistakes all over again.

Things You Should Know

We cannot predict or control the future, but the more clearly we imagine the future, the better we can plan for it. By planning for the future and do things to help it happen, we reduce our anxiety and enjoy our lives even more.

When you focus on the right things, you will have enough energy and confidence to handle the most difficult situations.

Think of the impact we would have if we can convince half of the population to stop abusing their credit cards. Not only will we reduce wastage but also improve our money matters.

We also have the buying power to stop the world worst polluters and make them clean up their mess by stop buying their products until they comply with our demands.

We have to redouble our efforts, work intensively to inform, educate, organise and build a social force that can stop the environment crisis on our planet. We have to lead a global fight against ecological destruction and keep the politicians and industrialists accountable for their actions.

Flood media outlets, corporate executives and government officials with information about the coming financial crisis and inform them what's really going on in the world.

What are your options?

1. Do nothing if you believe that the economic crisis we are facing will be over in five years and will not have any serious impact on our living standards . It is good to be an optimist however, I doubt it very much that you have read my whole book.

2. Try to take on the establishment all by yourself. The very wealthy has control over the main media and brought neoliberalism into existence to protect their wealth. Therefore you will fail.

3. Form solidarity networks as a means of building resistance to austerity. People reading this book and other relevant books will rise up and take control. I believe the time is now. For those of us who are interested not only in our basic survival but ending extreme inequality, and planetary destruction we have to increase our collective power. By building social networks informing them about the coming financial crisis and how to prepare for it will boost your morale and confidence. History has proved that groups with large following were powerful enough to change things. More members would provide more experience, more power, and be better prepared to launch effective action plans.

The ultimate aim is of course the nationalisation of our Reserve Banks and to let the bank barons who steals from us face justice.

For the risk takers

If you are not already prepared, it will be wise to invest in a lifestyle block which would ensure that you and your family are self-sustained regarding power, heat, food and water. It is also advisable to invest in transport which does not require gasoline or diesel.

See yourself in a rural area with a nice veggie garden, some friendly chickens, collection facilities for rainwater and a few photocells for electricity. Rain would periodically fall. The chickens would lay eggs as usual and the sun would continue to shine.

For everyone else

Change of mindset

1) Resist groupthink: investigating against the crowd requires more than just thinking for yourself. The tendency to conform is not strictly an intellectual process but largely emotional.

2) Error of short-sightedness; develop an open mind accepting that situations are always changing, and be willing to acknowledge that the recent past is not necessarily an accurate guide to the future.

3) Open-minded; you must learn to think for yourself, and be unswayed by emotion.

4) Spot the dangers and prepare yourself.

5) Stay in control don't panic.

6) React quickly, the time it takes to respond can make a huge difference.

7) Learn negotiating skills.

<u>Planning</u>

1) Be prepared, prepare for the bad time ahead and you will only know good times.

2) Have a roof over your head.

3) Learn new skills and be more marketable (how to make candles/soap, husbandry).

4) Improve your health: be fit, diet.

5) Gather useful information on what to do in a

crisis.

6) Make a list of what you need and don't need.

7) Make a list of who to contact and what to do.

Finances

1) Start a side business.

2) If possible stock gold and silver, buy small denominations.

3) Pay off as much of your debt as possible. Pay off your credit card.

4) Sell all your bonds.

5) Reduce spending: starting right now.

6) Try to sell life insurance as the value of life insurance with high inflation will not be worth much in the future.

7) Get rid of all the insurances you don't need.

8) If you are renting furniture, appliances or anything besides the roof over your head, then *give it back.*

Culture and community

1) Improve community alliances (friends and family for support and defence.

2) Change our culture and learn that higher consumption is immoral.
3) Learn to cooperate more with people from different cultures.
4) Be kind to the people you love.
5) Don't hide in shame.

Production

1) If possible move to a rural area.
2) Must have plan of production for long term food supplies.

Gather supplies

a) Cash
Keep enough cash to last a couple of months

b) Medical supplies (first aid kit)
Plasters   Scissors
Bandages   Pain tablets
Cotton   Tweezers

c) Water
Collect and store water in containers.
Collect water from roof.
Have two means of purify water.
Boil, filter, bleach,

Things You Should Know

d) Fire
Wood
Matches, lighters, stick lighters

e) Equipment
Led flash light	Axe
Radio	Corded phone
Batteries	Knives
Gloves	Weapons
Can openers	Duct tape
Mouse traps	Rubbish bags

f) Clothes
Warm clothes	Boots for walking
Rain coats	Blankets
Backpacks

g) Food
Rice	Dry beans
Cans of fruit	Cans of fish and meat
Cans of vegetables	Peanut butter
Boxes of drink mix	Flour
Sugar	Oats
Olive oil	Pet food
Vitamin supplies	Seed
Honey	Vinegar

h) Personal items
Razors	Soap
Deodorant	Tooth paste
Toilet paper	Bleach
Sanitation	Hygiene items

Top barter items

1) Precious metals

2) Ammunition

3) Water and purification methods

4) Seeds

5) Food

6) Fuel

7) Batteries

Methods to safeguard your wealth

1) Exit the stock market.

2) Stay away from real estate till well in the after-shock.

3) Stay away from long term bonds.

Precious metals and stones

Gold holds an unusual position in the minds of many people around the world as a store of monetary value. Gold is very small compared to the stock and bond markets. Even a small shift of capital out of these markets and

Things You Should Know

into the gold market, will dramatic boost its price. Historically, silver has more or less tracked gold trends up and down.

The demand for gold as jewellery will fall since jewellery is a discretionary good.

Gold and silver is not a buy and forget investment, as the future would be in a very dynamic changing economy.

Precious gem stones come in two general varieties: investment grade and non-investment grade. The high quality gems will do very well in the downturn.

Facts about precious metals;

Precious metals are not very magnetic.

Silver melts ice fast.

The density of tungsten is very close to that of gold.

Now that you have a plan, put some things in place and are better prepared for any forth coming crisis, it is time to stop thinking all about gloom and doom. Give yourself permission to worry less and enjoy more. You've earned it. Go and enjoy life that is what really matters.

Here is some ways to give to the community;

1) Time: this is one of the most valuable gift of all. It is precious and increasingly scares amid the fast pace of modern life.

2) Knowledge: sharing knowledge with others is a great way to give as it does not matter whether you are rich or poor.

3) Blessings: giving blessings of approval or support always makes everyone feel better.

4) Thanks: expressions of gratitude are always appreciated in any circumstances.

5) Money: it seems a poor substitute for all the above but it can work wonders.

40. Keywords

Active income; active income is derived from salary, or net operating earnings if you are self- employed.

Aftershock: Is the second phase of the popping of the bubble economy. Just when many people think the worst is over, then comes the Aftershock, when the dollar bubble and government debt bubble will burst.

Assets: A tangible thing that is owned and worth

money, such as a person owning a house.

Bank: an institution that offers various financial services.

Banknote: a note issued by a bank, which serves as money.

Bankrupt; unable to pay one's debt, insolvent, having liabilities in excess of a reasonable market value of assets held.

Basel Accord: a set of regulations that established levels of bank capital, drawn up by the Basel Committee on Banking Supervision. The first accord, known as Basel I was drawn up in 1988. In 2004 a Basel II accord was published that was designed to align bank capital with risk in a closer manner.

Bear: A falling market, or a person who predicts one.

Bond: an interest bearing certificate redeemable on a specified date used by companies and governments to raise capital by borrowing.

Broker: an agent who negotiates contracts of purchase and sale: a power broker.

Bubble: an illusory inflation in price that is grossly out of proportion to underlying values.

Budget: an estimate of income and expenditure within specified limits.

Bull market: A period of sustained increases in overall stock prices.

Business cycle: a predictable long-term pattern of alternating periods of economic growth (recovery) and decline (recession).

Capital gains: appreciation in the price or value of an asset. Capital gains are generally realised when the asset is sold, until then they are referred to as paper gains.

Capital Market Liberalisation: A controversial aspect of globalisation. It is the policy of opening up markets to rapid movement of foreign capital. It is a strategy advocated by market fundamentalist such as the IMF.

Capitalism: an economic system in which trade and industry are controlled by private owners for profit. In order for capitalism to work people need to invest in order for others to borrow.

Capitalization: market value of a company's stock

Cartel: a combination of producers of any product joined together to control its production, sale and price, so as to obtain a monopoly and restrict competition in that industry or commodity.

Cash Flow: is the currency flow. It is negative if it flows out your pocket like when you're spending. Positive cash flow happens from an asset that produces more cash than expenses.

Central bank: a non-commercial bank, which may or may not be independent of government, which has some or all of the following functions: conduct monetary policy: oversee the stability of the financial system: issue currency notes: act as a banker to the government; supervise financial institutions and regulate payment systems.

Collateralised Debt Obligation, (CDO's): a form of asset-backed security. They are typically created by bundling together a portfolio of fixed-income debt and using those assets to back the issuance of notes. Such notes usually carry varying levels of risks.

Communism: a social system in which property is owned by the community and each member works for the common benefit.

Compound interest: interest calculated not only on the initial principal but on the accumulated interest of prior payment periods.

Consume: to destroy: to use up: to eat up or drink up: to waste away.

Consumerism: the protection of consumers' interest

Credit: The potential to receive loans, or, the faith of another.

Credit cards: is a steal from your future item. For most people a credit card is like poison in their hands and the vultures do their best to sell you more credit cards and keep you in debt.

Credit Default Swap (CDS) A contract between two parties, where the buyers pays a regular fee to the seller in exchange for a guarantee that they will be compensated in the case of any default on a stipulated piece of debt. It is similar to insurance but not strictly regulated and can be freely traded.

Currency: money in any form when in use as medium of exchange, facilitating the transfer of goods and services.

Currency wars: is a policy to deliberately weaken your own currency. This happens when central banks reduce the attractiveness of holding cash.

Default: Unable to repay your debts.

Deflation; ICE a general decline in prices, often caused by a reduction in the supply of money. Deflation has the side effect of increased unemployment. Deflation is a decline in assets.

Deregulation: the process of removing government controls from the market and increasing free trade.

Derivative: a financial instrument whose characteristics and value depend upon the characteristics and value of a bond, equity or currency. Familiar examples of derivatives include "futures" and "options".

Disaster: devastating and sudden misfortune: utter failure.

Diversified: Investment selected to represent a variety of asset classes or industries to spread or lower the risk of the portfolio.

Equity: Ownership, the amount that your assets are more than your liabilities.

Equity funding: A method of accessing investment money through the sale of shares in the enterprise accepting responsibility for the investment.

Federal Reserve banks of U.S: The banks that carry out Federal Reserve operations, including controlling the money supply and regulating member banks. There are 12 District Feds, with headquarters in

Boston, New York, Philadelphia, Cleveland, St Louis, San Francisco, Richmond, Atlanta, Chicago, Minneapolis, Kansas City, and Dallas.

Fiat: Latin for "let it be done;" an arbitrary order or decree.

Fiat money: Legal tender, especially paper currency, authorized by a government but not based on or convertible into gold or silver.

Financial repression: when governments reduce their debt and steal the wealth of the savers, they do it by: a) capping of interest rates, b) forcing companies to buy government bonds, c) exerting government control over banks and Social security funds.

Fiscal policy: The way in which government uses public spending and taxation to influence a country's economic performance.

Floating exchange rate: a foreign exchange rate that is not fixed by national authorities, but varies according to supply and demand.

Gambling; gambling houses emphasize action and activity all geared to create excitement and the expectation of big wins. It offers you the prospects of increasing your money without much effort. If you lose you have nothing to show for it. Their goal is to separate you from your money and the odds are on their side.

Globalisation; the tendency of business, technologies or philosophies to spread throughout the world exerting tremendous downward pressure on the price of manufacturing goods due to rapid increase in cheap produced goods with cheap labour.

Gold standard: a monetary system in which currency is convertible into fixed amounts of gold.

Gross Domestic Product (GDP): the market value of all goods and services in their final use that are produced within a country during a specified period, it is a measure of income.

Hedge Fund: a fund that invests people's money for them and receives a performance fee. By being somewhat exclusive in choosing investors, hedge funds do not fall under existing classification, so they are free to implement riskier investment strategies than mutual funds.

Hyperinflation; (FIRE) occurs when a country experience very high and usually accelerating rates of monetary and price inflation causing the population to minimise their holdings of money. Hyperinflation is out of control inflation and price increases is out of control. During Germany's hyperinflation prices doubled every 28 hours.

Index: Assets bound together so they can reflect the market as a whole.

Inflation: is an increase in the price of goods and services NOT due to growing demand or shrinking supply for those goods and services but due to money losing its buying power. Prices go up because buying power of money goes down. Inflation is caused by excess increase in money supply.

Bad economies have high inflation as the government has difficulty raising money from taxes. Hence, it has to resort to inflation to obtain the money it wants.

Infrastructure: the set of interconnected structural elements that provide the framework for supporting the entire structure.

Interest: money paid for the use of money lent.

Insider trading: buying or selling a security based on information that has not been released to the public (inside information). An insider is usually defined as an officer, director, or key employee, but can include family members or others. Inside trading is illegal.

Insolvency: the inability of a person or organisation to pay financial obligations as they become due.

International Monetary Fund (IMF): an international organisation meant to strengthen developing economies by offering policy advice, loans and monitoring of a nation's economy. Its goal is especially to prevent unpredictable changes in exchange rates, in which countries harm one another. It regulates, advises free exchange of currency, rather than exchange controls.

Investment: the purchase, construction, or development of capital resources. Investments increase the supply of capital. You buy something and get paid for owning it. Investment is not speculation.

Kleptocracy: a government in which corruption is endemic; taxes and other government funds are used for personal profit of officials, at the expense of the wider populace.

Leverage: The use of debt to finance a financial

problem.

Liabilities: money or debt owed to another person or identity, including loans, taxes, and judgments.

Liquidity: An asset that can easily and quickly be converted to purchasing power without loss of value such as cash and money in the bank.

Liquidity trap: is when the usual rules of economics don't apply. Liquidity trap is an extended recession that suppresses velocity.

Market: An abstract concept that encompasses the trading arrangements of buyers and sellers that underlie the forces of supply and demand.

Monetary Policy: The trading of government securities to change the supply of money, as opposed to *fiscal policy*. Monetary policy can complement or conflict with fiscal policy.

Money: the assets that is commonly used to pay for things; the medium of exchange most commonly used by buyers and sellers.

Monopolies: exclusive possession of the sale of some commodity or service.

Mortgage: loan used to buy a home or commercial property, secured by the property.

Mutual fund: arrangement in which investment professionals accept money from the public, pool the money into a fund with specific investment objectives, and manage the fund and administration details.

Negative Equity: owning more money on a loan that

a house would sell for. A person with a negative equity is likely to default and a high risk for the banks.

Neoliberalism: a strand of economic thinking that believe in privatising government assets, reduce government spending, reducing tax, and remove barriers to trade. Neo-liberalism arose in the 1970's as a response to the regulatory mechanism that were in place as result of large-scale battles between workers with their unions and other forms of worker organisations and the owners (capitalists) by removing state intervention from markets and decimating social programs for workers and allowing capital to move across borders. Their aim is to destroy the unions. It is thus the ruling class' offensive against the working class to improve their austerity.

Net worth: value of the assets of a person, business, or other entity minus the value of their liabilities.

Oligarchy: government by a few, usually the rich, for their own advantage.

Oligopolies: a situation in which a particular market is controlled by a small group of firms.

Passive income; refers to recurring cash flow derived from income producing assets.

Ponzi scheme; the essence of a Ponzi scheme is deception. The investor thinks that the promised high return on his investment will come from the promoter's putting the investment to work, not that his investment will be used to pay other investors in order to keep the scheme going.

Profit: an excess of returns over outlay.

Pyramid scheme; where a person pays a fee to become a retail seller of a product and is promised a fee of any other retail seller whom he recruits. Eventually there are no more recruits, and that is what happens in a speculative bubble, which must eventually stop expanding and then burst.

Quantitative easing: is when central banks create money to influence the economy rather than through raising or lowering interest rates.

Recession: A socio-economic environment in which the total of income generated falls behind established value.

Rent seeking; refers to propensity of entrepreneurs to concentrate their efforts on obtaining protection and subsidies.

Socialism: a political and economic theory advocating that land, transport, natural resources and the chief industries should be owned and managed by the State. In order for socialism to work the wealthy have to give a portion of their wealth to the government to hand it over to the poor.

Short sales: selling assets (house) for less than the loan (mortgage), with the lenders approval.

Short-selling; the speculator sells a stock he doesn't own by borrowing some stock to give to the buyer. Then he buys back the stock in the market, hopefully at a lower price, and delivers it to the party he borrowed from.

Speculation: is buying an asset because you hope

that you will be able to sell it for more at some later date.

Sub-prime mortgages: the term is applied to loans that carry a higher-than-normal risk of default such as loans to borrowers with low credit scores.

Supply and demand: the fundamental model of a market economy. It stipulates that the greater the demand for a product the higher the price will be, until supply outstrips demand. At this point, the price will fall until an equilibrium is achieved between quantity and price.

Usury: the practice of lending money and charging the borrower interest at an exorbitant or illegally high rate.

U.S Treasury; usually low risk, low reward backed by the full faith and credit of the U.S. government.

World Bank: International Bank for Reconstruction and Development. The World Bank funds reconstruction in developing nations. It is not the IMF. Few people can tell the difference.

World Trade Organisation: an International organisation which administers multilateral agreements defining the rules of international trade between its member states.

41. Bibliography

Alan Bollard, *Crisis*, Auckland University Press, 2010.

Amanda Morral, *Money matters*, Penguin Books, 2013

A.N Field, *The truth about New Zealand*, Veritas Publishing Co 1987

Benjamin J. Cohen, *Currency Power, understanding monetary rivalry*, Princeton University Press 2015.

Brent Kessel, *It's not About the Money*, HarperCollins 2009

Charles Ferguson, *Inside job*, A Oneworld Book, 2012

Charles Ferguson, *Predator Nation* crown Publishing, 2012

Corey Rosenbloom, *The complete trading course*, John Wiley & Sons Inc. 2011

Dr.Chin-Yun Lin, *Money Vitals*, PublishMe, 2010

Daniel R Solin *The smartest money book*, Penguin Group 2012

David Weidemer, PHD, *Aftershock*, John Wiley & sons Inc. 2011

Elizabeth Warren & Amelia Warren Tyagi, *All your*

worth, Free Press 2005

Ellen Hodgson Brown, J.D. *The Web of Debt*, Third Millennium Press 2008

Fintan O' Tool, *Ship of Fools*, Faber and Faber Ltd. 2010

Gary Belsky & Thomas Gilovich, *Why smart people make big money mistakes*, Simon & Schuster paperbacks 2009

George Walden, *China A wolf in the World?*, 1988

Gillian Tett. *Fool's Gold*, Little Brown, 2009

Harry S. Dent Jr. *The demographic cliff*, Portfolio/Penguin, 2014

Jack Ablin, *Reading Minds and Markets*, Pearson Education , Inc 2009

James D. Gwartney & Richard L. Stroup & Dwight R. Lee & Tawni H. Ferrarini,

Common Sense Economics, Martin's Press 2010

James Richards Currency wars, Penguin Group 2011

James Turk & John Rubino, *The Money Bubble*, DollarCollapse Press, 2013

Jim Brit, *Do this. Get Rich!*, Square One Publishers 2007

Joe Studwell, *How Asia Works*, Profile Books 2013

John Cassidy, *How Markets fail*, Farrar, Straus and Giroux 2009

John Mauldin & Jonathan Tepper,John , *Code Red*, John Wiley & Sons Inc. 2014

Joseph E. Stiglitz & Andrew Charlton. *Fair trade for all*, Oxford University Press 2005

Joseph E, Stiglitz, *Freefall*, Penguin Group, 2010.

Justin Fox, *The myth of the rational market*, HarperCollins 2009

Kishore Mahbubani, *The great convergence*, PublicAffairs, Perseus Books, 2013

Les Hunter, *Courage to change*, Harbourside Publications Limited, 2002

Martin Hawes, *Twenty good summers*, Allen & Unwin 2012

Mary Hunt, *7 Money rules for life*, Revell 2012

Max Borders, *Super Wealth*, Throne 2012

Michael J. Casey, *The unfair Trade*, Crown Publishing Group 2012

Michael Lewis, *Panic*, Penguin books 2008

Mitch Feierstein, *Planet Ponzi*, Transworld Publishers 2012

Peter Aranyi, *How to Survive and prosper in a Falling Property Market*, Publishing Press Ltd. 2008

Peter Sander, *The 25 habits of highly successful investors*, Adams Media 2013

Philip Coggan, *Paper Promises*, Penguin Group 2011

Richard A. Posner, *A Failure of Capitalism*, Harvard University Press 2009

Richard H. Thaler & Cass R. Sunstein *Nudge*, Yale University Press, 2008

Robert Brenner, *The Boom and the Bubble*, Verso 2002

Robert Peston & Laurence Knight, *How do we fix this mess?*, Hodder& Stoughton 2012

Robert T Kiyosaki *Rich Dad's Conspiracy of The Rich*, Hachette Book Group, Inc. 2009

Rodney King, *The Singapore Miracle*, Insight Press 2008

Roger Boyes, *Meltdown Iceland*, Bloomsbury 2009

Stephan Mitford Goodson, *A History of Central Banking and the Enslavement of Mankind*, Black House Publishing Ltd, 2014.

Stephan R Covey, *The 3rd Alternative*, Simon & Schuster 2011

Stephen Leeb, The Coming Economic Collapse, Warner Business Books, 2006

Steve Keen, *Debunking Economics*, Zedbooks 2011

Timothy Ferris, *The 4-hour work week*, Random House Group Company 2007

Thom Hartmann, *The crash of 2016*, Twelve Hachette Book Group 2013

Wikipedia, the free encyclopaedia.

André Klopper

ABOUT THE AUTHOR

André Klopper was born in Krugersdorp, South Africa. He is married and has two daughters. He worked as a Finance Manager for twelve years in Pretoria for a large telecommunication company before emigrating to New Zealand in 2000. He spends his time researching for his next book, and loves taking long walks.

www.ingramcontent.com/pod-product-compliance
Lightning Source LLC
Chambersburg PA
CBHW071355170526
45165CB00001B/52